Improving Behaviour Management in Your School

Improving Behaviour Management in Your School provides a common-sense approach to understanding the causes and triggers of students' challenging behaviour and equips teachers and school leaders with simple tools that can be easily implemented in any school. In his accessible and upbeat style, Tim Dansie uses case studies throughout the book which draw on strategies based on CBT and mindfulness. These strategies have proven to make a huge difference to school life and to how challenging students are managed. Teachers are encouraged to question how schools and classrooms are structured, in order to create environments where all students have the greatest possible opportunity to learn and grow as individuals. This resource includes accessible chapters about:

- What are challenging behaviours?
- What are the causes of challenging behaviours in students?
- How to work with parents
- How to get staff on board.

This is a must-read for all practising and training teachers who wish to understand the reasons for challenging behaviour and how to improve it.

Tim Dansie is a freelance education consultant, registered psychologist and teacher. He delivers seminars and training sessions across Australia on managing behaviour.

Improving Behaviour Management in Your School

Creating calm spaces for pupils to learn and flourish

Tim Dansie

Routledge
Taylor & Francis Group

LONDON AND NEW YORK

First published 2017
by Routledge
2 Park Square, Milton Park, Abingdon, Oxon OX14 4RN

and by Routledge
711 Third Avenue, New York, NY 10017

Routledge is an imprint of the Taylor & Francis Group, an informa business

© 2017 T. Dansie

British Library Cataloguing in Publication Data
A catalogue record for this book is available from the British Library

Library of Congress Cataloging in Publication Data
Names: Dansie, Tim, author.
Title: Improving behaviour management in your school : creating calm spaces for pupils to learn and flourish / Tim Dansie.
Description: New York, NY : Routledge, 2016.
Identifiers: LCCN 2016024037 | ISBN 9781138654068 (hardback) | ISBN 9781138654075 (pbk.) | ISBN 9781315623443 (ebook)
Subjects: LCSH: Classroom management. | School discipline. | Problem children--Behavior modification. | Motivation in education.
Classification: LCC LB3013 .D358 2016 | DDC 371.102/4--dc23
LC record available at https://lccn.loc.gov/2016024037

ISBN: 978-1-138-65406-8 (hbk)
ISBN: 978-1-138-65407-5 (pbk)
ISBN: 978-1-315-62344-3 (ebk)

Typeset in Adobe Garamond Pro
by Saxon Graphics Ltd, Derby

Contents

Contents

1 Introduction

Hello, my name is Tim Dansie and thank you for taking the time to read *Improving Behaviour Management in Your School: Creating calm spaces for pupils to learn and flourish*. I must be completely honest and say that I was one of the challenging students so often presenting in the classroom today. As a result of my own personal experiences at school, I have become passionate about helping teachers and students in learning how to cope within the school and classroom environment.

I was the student who developed the many avoidance strategies needed to survive through school. If I had a maths test on a Thursday I would rub my head against the pillowcase and then complain to my parents of feeling unwell. They would put a hand to my forehead and feel that I was hot and suggest that I stay home from school. That evening, I would ring my friends up and get the answers. Alternatively, I would get the answers to assignments from my friends before school. This worked well until the introduction of exams. As a result I left school at the age of 16 wanting to be a professional sportsman. After earning $25 in four years I decided it wasn't a great career move and reconsidered my future.

At the age of 21, I returned to study and it was through my study that I learnt that I had the specific learning difficulty dysgraphia. This was why I found aspects of learning so challenging and my behaviours at school reflected my difficulty. I wasn't a disruptive student but a disengaged student who avoided work at all costs.

Now at the time of writing I have completed a Diploma of Teaching, a Bachelor of Education, a Graduate Diploma of Psychology, a Masters of Psychology and I am a member of the Australian Psychological Society. I maintain my registration as a teacher and psychologist and I have spent 12 years as a teacher in schools and 14 years in private practice as a psychologist, predominantly working in schools. Not bad for a high school drop-out!

In this book I hope to provide you with an understanding of why we are seeing more and more challenging behaviours presenting in schools, the causes of the challenging behaviours and most importantly some strategies that can be put into place to help teachers, schools, students and parents manage the behaviours. I will share with you some of my observations of schools, but also case studies of some of the students I have worked with in the last ten years.

I think as a starting point we must consider why schools have changed so much over the last 25 years and why we are seeing more and more challenging behaviours.

So many theories, so many experts, so much information, leading to so much confusion

How schools have changed over the past 25 years! So many theories, philosophies and behavioural management techniques have passed through schools, yet still schools are being challenged by children who have great behavioural and learning needs. I always question why this is the case, given that we now know so much more about the development of children and how learning happens.

What is it that has changed in society that has impacted upon schooling, teaching and the behaviour of students to such an extent?

- **Family breakdown**
  More and more students are living in single-parent families or blended families and this is a common catalyst for challenging behaviour for students. Students come to school each day with uncertainty, grief and confusion about rules and routines, due to not having any or too many rules and routines in the houses in which they live.

- **Change in the approach to discipline**
  Many of today's parents have moved well away from an authoritarian style of parenting, due to rejecting this style that they experienced as children. What we now see are parents who do not enforce boundaries, rules or consequences, again leading to very confused children, as at school there are boundaries, rules and consequences. Unfortunately, parents are often very poor role models for students, leading to a student showing similar behaviours to those of their parents.

- **Parents'/society's expectation of schools has changed**
  Parents, and to some extent society, are dictating that schools need to raise students rather than purely teach them. Many parents I

meet have the belief that it is not only the school's responsibility to teach their child, but to also 'fix the behaviour'.

- **Changes in school structures**
When I first started teaching, the classes were streamed into three sets: A, B and C. The A set had the most students in the class, while the B and C sets had smaller numbers of students, with the C set receiving the most extra learning support. Today here in Australia, schools do not have streaming, rather it is up to the teacher to differentiate the curriculum to meet the needs of the entire class, which given the range of abilities within a class is a great challenge. Furthermore, gone are the majority of the traditional Australian trade schools which allowed students to attend a school which prepared them for working life and really catered for the students who had specific learning disabilities. It seems the push is for every student to complete their final year of school and then to progress into further education.

Another change in school structures is the reduction in the numbers of schools specifically designed for students whose behaviours caused such a disruption to the classroom environment that they could not attend the mainstream school or for students whose learning/functioning needs were so great that they could not be cared for in a mainstream school. This has resulted in more and more students being left in schools that do not have the resources to cater for them properly.

- **Curricula with far too much in them**
So many teachers tell me that teaching is no longer fun. The demands of meeting the curriculum are just too great, which leads to fun activities and lessons being shelved. As a part of this, teachers also state that there is now such an excessive amount of paperwork, reporting and over-governing in schools that it is too hard to do fun activities. I have seen the steady decline in wonderful school-based activities such as camps, excursions, sport, musicals or drama performances due to factors such as health and safety, police clearances, political correctness and the fear of litigation. The end result is that students miss out, and teachers are caused excessive stress.

- **Greater understanding of mental health**

  We now have so much more information at our fingertips and schools, teachers and parents now know so much more about conditions which impact upon the behaviour of our children. The difficulty is that teachers now have to be psychologists, occupational therapists, speech pathologists, psychiatrists, doctors (how many teachers give medicine to children?), as well as teachers. I see this as a major shift in the view of teachers, but also the expectations placed on them.

- **Specific learning disabilities**

  Our knowledge has increased enormously about how students learn. Teachers are now required to cater for the individual learning needs of the entire class, while differentiating the curriculum to meet the needs of the different ranges of overall abilities of the class. Again, so much is required of our teachers.

- **Schools as businesses**

  With ever-changing funding models, some schools are now under pressure to keep students at school or to attract students to their school. Funding is now a constant restraint in so many schools, which leads to lack of support for students who need it the most.

- **School involvement**

  This is a passion of mine, but I am sad to see the lack of extra-curricular activities offered in Australian schools. I grew up playing sport for my school in summer and winter and, although we had parents predominantly coaching our teams, they were totally supported by the school. Friday afternoon was always interschool sport coached by teachers and as students we looked forward to it and loved it. Bring back interschool sport into schools on Friday afternoons, as it develops school pride, a sense of belonging to a team, but also an incentive for students to behave well during the week.

Finally, it has become so confusing for teachers, school administrators and parents alike as to what rules/laws actually apply to students who have challenging behaviours. There are many legislative acts, laws and policies that all have an implication in the management of children with challenging behaviours in schools. An example of some of the Acts that apply here in Australia are as follows:

- The Human Rights Act
- United Nations Convention on the Rights of Persons with Disabilities
- Education Act
- Commonwealth Disability Discrimination Act
- Disability Standards of Education
- Discrimination Act
- Work, Health and Safety Act
- Information Privacy Act
- Health Records (Privacy and Access) Act
- Children and Young People Act
- Domestic Violence and Protection Orders Act
- Working with Vulnerable People Act
- Australian Curriculum
- National Safe School Framework
- Parent Engagement in Children's Learning Program
- Student Resilience and Well-being Policy
- National Education reform Agreement.

Countries such as the UK, the USA and New Zealand also have similar legislation relating to education and it is the sheer volume of legislation that causes so much confusion for schools administrators, teachers and parents alike.

In my view, a significant cause of the confusion is the language that is often used in the documents. Too often I read words such as 'reasonable' and 'justifiable' and this leads to many questions. Unfortunately, what a parent who has a child with challenging behaviour perceives as reasonable can be markedly different to what a teacher perceives as reasonable, and this is again different to what a principal or parent of another student in the classroom perceives as being reasonable. Some of the legislation conflicts, leading to an unclear understanding of the process of how to manage a student with challenging behaviours.

Schools have changed dramatically and there is no doubt that there is so much more pressure on teachers and school administrators. But the behaviour of students has also changed. All of this has made managing behaviours in schools a great challenge and one that our teachers need to have more and more support to do. Bearing this in mind, I think it is a good time to reflect on what a school in a perfect world looks like. Before reading on, put a bookmark in and create a list for yourself of what you believe the perfect school looks like and how it manages challenging behaviours. After five minutes, open up the book, read on and compare your ideas to mine. I trust we are thinking the same way.

In a perfect world, what does a school look like?

My belief is that in a perfect world every child has an equal opportunity to learn, which leads to my classroom mantra – 'as long as a child's behaviour does not impact upon the learning environment or opportunities of the other students in the class, the classroom is a good place'. If behaviour is impacting upon the learning of others, then action needs to occur. Unfortunately, in many classrooms today this is the case, and more and more teachers are becoming frustrated because they spend 95 per cent of their time managing, say, one to three children (sometimes more), while the other class members simply go about their work.

I recently visited a Year 3 classroom of 27 students. Within the class there was a student who was diagnosed with attention deficit hyperactivity disorder (ADHD) and was not on medication due to their parents' beliefs; a student diagnosed as being on the autism spectrum (ASD – autism spectrum disorder); a student diagnosed as having oppositional defiance disorder (ODD); two students with dyslexia and a student diagnosed as having a central auditory processing disorder (CAP-D). The teacher spent the majority of her time trying to manage the students with ADHD, ASD and ODD, while the students with dyslexia and CAP-D battled on with minimal learning support. The remaining class members received little or no individual contact with the teacher.

When talking to the teacher it was clear that she was stressed, feeling unsupported and at a loss as to what to do. Very strong feelings of guilt were also present as the teacher felt that she was not teaching her class, but just managing three students to the best of her ability. This made me think – what do teachers want/need to be able to teach their class, allow for individual learning needs and manage challenging behaviours? What happens in a perfect world of teaching, a perfect school?

I recently asked a group of teachers this question: In a perfect world what would you have or have happening in your school to manage challenging behaviours? The responses were:

- More staff support for students with behavioural needs.
- Schools designed for students with challenging behaviours.
- Classrooms designed to help students with challenging behaviours.
- Cooperative timetabling to allow students to be withdrawn, so extra learning support is available.
- Less curriculum-driven focus for children with behavioural needs.
- A greater understanding of students' conditions.
- More professional development.
- More external professional support.
- Better understanding from parents.
- Better understanding from fellow staff.
- A whole-school approach to managing behaviours.
- A school where the teachers' well-being is considered.

What does this mean? How can the above be implemented in a school? Let's look at each one of the above in more detail with some ideas that could be applied.

More staff support for students with behavioural needs

Having visited hundreds of schools there is no doubt in my mind that schools are crying out for a behavioural specialist who is there to support teachers, coordinate programmes, engage external professionals, educate parents and external support staff from within the community and to create an environment where children feel safe. This is the perfect world I am talking about, but also something to aspire to. Unfortunately, at present in most schools this role falls to the learning support coordinator or principal, neither of whom have time due to the roles/duties they already have. So this then creates the question, who can support teachers?

The obvious choice is the immediate school community being made up of parents, grandparents, retired teachers or people within the community who have a connection to the school and are willing to help. (Please see Appendix 2 on how to engage parents in schools.) The critical factor is teaching/preparing any volunteer to be able to work in a classroom, with a small group or on a one-to-one basis, and this is done through ongoing professional development. In a perfect world, students who have behavioural needs will have an ongoing rapport with a significant person at school who is not their immediate teacher, but who has time and space to be able to sit down and work with a student or group of students. But before we do this, what we need to do is create the environment for students where they are safe, but most importantly motivated to learn.

Schools designed for students with challenging behaviours

So we now have a behavioural team at school, but what is the point of having the team if they do not have a space to work in? In a perfect world, schools would have a space which is specifically designed for students who have challenging behaviours and this space takes into account the learning needs of students with challenging behaviours.

What does this space look like? The most important component of this space is that students can feel safe, thus the first thing is to have kind and caring staff. Staff working in the CBS (Challenging Behaviour Space) are well trained, aware of the specific needs of children and have the resources available to support students. They also have the ability to have fun and make learning fun.

In the CBS there is the following:

- Computers/tablets that have games and learning programs that engage students.
- Items such as a trampoline, punching bag, pillows etc., that students can use to express anger and frustration.
- A Wii Fit to be used as fun, but also to develop sensory and motor skills.
- Sensory items to hold, fiddle with or lie down on.
- Soft toys to cuddle and hold when upset.
- Animals such as fish or even a dog to care for.
- Activities to stimulate thinking such as Lego, jigsaw puzzles, building blocks etc.
- A variety of furniture to utilise while learning.

- Food and drinks (healthy choices, of course).
- Staff that understand students and who have skills in counselling.

The room needs to be set up to have the wow factor, so students are happy and feel safe in the environment.

Contrary to this we could have entire schools that are purely for students who have challenging behaviours. My personal belief is that this is not ideal, as I think it is important for all students to be in their local school or school of parents' choice. Removing students from school and placing them in a school focused purely on behaviour change should only be a last resort.

Classrooms designed to help students with challenging behaviours

Classrooms are changing with the times. We are now moving away from the traditional structure of desks to learning environments where students stand, sit and/or lie down in rooms that may have between 15 and 90 students. With this, we also have more and more technology; students have tablets, laptops and books, and the classrooms have smart boards, televisions that link to iPads and sound systems. So what else do we need in the classroom environment?

- Teachers who know how to use the technology that is available to them. Too many teachers do not know or are unwilling to adapt their teaching methodologies to the times and as a result, learning is boring, which results in disruptive behaviours.
- Computer hubs with learning activities where students can go to do self-directed learning when frustrated, angry or on the edge of a meltdown.
- Places where students can go and sit to calm themselves, away from other students. Consider using tents, bean bags or even physio balls as an option.
- Teachers who accept students' learning needs and styles and who are prepared to let a student fiddle with an object. Remember, as long as a student is not disrupting the learning of others the classroom is a good place.

- Sensory objects placed around the room for students to hold or have.
- Objects like a trampoline the students can bounce on.
- Classrooms that have the wow factor. I once worked in a classroom where the theme for the term was surfing. There were surfboards hanging from the roof, posters of surfing on the walls, a sand area in the corner and Friday was often 'dress for the beach' day. It was cool and the students loved it.

Never underestimate the power of the learning environment when managing behaviour.

Cooperative timetabling to enable more effective teaching of all students, but also to manage students with behavioural needs better

CASE STUDY

I recently visited a school which had two Year 1 classes of 25 students (5 and 6 year olds). One class had three students and the other two students with quite significant behavioural needs that were impacting upon the learning of the entire class. What was of note was that a support person had been allocated to support the teachers of the class on an equal basis. What was happening was the school support person would only work with one class at a time and within the classroom environment, but regardless of this, the students with behavioural needs were still being disruptive. The solution was cooperative timetabling. This resulted in the two Year 1 classes doing literacy and numeracy at the same time with the school support person taking the students with behavioural needs out of the classroom to work on specifically designed learning tasks with them.

This created a win–win situation for all. The Year 1 teachers could work with their classes without disruption, the students with behavioural needs were receiving learning tasks which were set to their learning levels in a small group with learning support available, and teachers received double the amount of student support. Schools can help by ensuring they maximise the support they receive and this can be done by clever and inventive timetabling.

More often than not students with challenging behaviours have learning needs. One of the critical factors in preventing so many behaviours is to ensure students can access the curriculum. With so many young students it is evident that when they are doing play-based activities they are fine, but when having to do more formal learning, frustration builds and behaviour changes. With older students, so much disruptive behaviour is due to not being able to complete the work and not wanting to appear to be having difficulty in front of their peers. Why is it that so many of our top comedians have specific learning difficulties? To help students, schools can use the timetable to plan for learning/behavioural support when it is needed for all students.

Let's face the facts – the majority of schools lack the support that they need to manage the behavioural and learning needs of students. As a result of this, the use of support has to be planned very well. An example of this may be as follows:

Two Year 1 classes totalling 50 children, five of which have quite extensive behavioural needs related to learning. When teaching literacy and numeracy each day the classes are combined and placed into learning groups with the five children being placed in a group together and allocated a learning/behavioural support person. The curriculum is tailored to the needs of all the groups and set at the learning level of the participants. The five students with high-level needs may spend more time on computers or using programmes specifically designed to improve learning outcomes, but they are working in a small group to increase their chances of success, while the rest of the class can go about learning without distraction. This also allows the teacher to monitor the progress of all students with greater ease.

The debate about learning structures within a classroom is one that continues to rage. Many of the teachers I talk to want to be able to set groups based on ability in the core learning subjects, such as numeracy and literacy to maximise effectiveness of teaching and to bring in specialised support for children who, for whatever reason, find learning challenging. Personally, I would like to see schools do whatever it takes to support the teachers in being able to maximise the learning outcomes of all students. If this means setting groups based on ability (differentiating) so be it, but the basic fact is, every child should have the best opportunity to learn.

Consideration should also be given to timetabling extra computer lab time, more non-contact time and specialist lessons in the afternoons, rather than in the morning, for classes that have a high number of students with behavioural needs. This is pretty harsh, but a principal can list the classes in order of the hardest to teach through to the easiest to teach, based on the needs of the class. I can hear the uproar of 'all classes have challenges' etc., but let's face the facts, teachers know which classes are harder than others as do principals, so the sensible thing is to look after the more challenging classes better through the use of timetabling.

Less curriculum-driven focus for students with behavioural needs

A concern of mine is the state of curriculum-driven schools as more and more topics are being put into an already crowded curriculum. When I talk to teachers I find the general consensus is that schools need to go back to the very basics, with a much greater focus on the learning of literacy and numeracy. What is needed is a topic of social studies which incorporates history, geography, science and health, a healthy dose of PE with school sport a bonus on Friday afternoons, a second language, music/drama and art all being included, based on the topic being taught. Most importantly, central to the curriculum is the learning of literacy and numeracy. This all sounds easy; however, for the student with behavioural needs, meeting the demands of the curriculum is too often the catalyst for disruptive behaviour, so adjustments need to be made.

For some behavioural needs students, meeting the demands of the curriculum is the last thing on their mind as their home lives are so chaotic and just coping with getting to school is enough. What must be remembered is that many children with behavioural needs have experienced trauma of some kind and, as a result, they are simply not ready to settle down in a typical classroom and learn. Schools must be more flexible in adapting the curriculum to meet the needs of an individual child. If this means that a new student only spends a small amount of time in the classroom, so be it, but the most important thing is to achieve the aim of settling the student into school.

CASE STUDY

Juliet is eight years old and it has been reported by her teachers that she is a delightful yet quiet student who had been making good progress with the development of her literacy and numeracy skills at school. Juliet's teachers are now very concerned about her as her demeanour at school has changed significantly as a result of witnessing an extreme domestic violence incident between her mother and father. Juliet was now showing the following behaviours:

- Not wanting to go to school; instead, wanting to stay home with her mum.
- Becoming very scared if routines were changed at school.
- Not wanting to leave the classroom to move to another classroom.
- Needing to have a soft toy to hold at all times when in the classroom.
- Only entering the classroom with her mother.
- Only leaving the classroom at the end of the day when her mother entered the room.
- Not wanting to talk about her father.
- Showing fear of her father coming to school to take her away.

In this case it was clearly evident that Juliet needed external professional counselling. However, Juliet's teachers were uncertain as to how best they could help her. It was recommended that the school and teachers implement these strategies to help Juliet:

- Set up a safe place in the classroom where Juliet can sit when feeing anxious.
- Have classwork for Juliet to do but remove pressure to complete the work.
- Provide as much one-to-one learning support in the classroom as possible – from teacher, student support officer, older peer or class buddy.
- Have self-directed learning activities available for Juliet on the computer or iPad.
- Have the daily routine written on a board for Juliet to see.

- Walk with Juliet on transitions from class to class.
- Allow Juliet to keep a toy at school to hold.
- Have staff monitor Juliet at break and lunchtime play.

The important thing in the case of Juliet was for the school to modify the curriculum and to make Juliet feel safe. Juliet was initially not ready to be focusing on the curriculum; rather her focus was on learning to feel safe again.

Schools need to be a safe place for students and adapting the curriculum to meet the needs of a student helps to make it safer!

A greater understanding of students' conditions

A great challenge for teachers is to get their head around and understand so many of the diagnosed conditions students are presenting with that lead to behavioural challenges within a classroom. Within any given classroom there is likely to be at least three students who have a diagnosis of some kind. Throw in some students who have specific learning difficulties and this means an awful lot of extra learning and adaptions for a teacher.

Teachers need the time to be able to learn more about students' needs, work with behavioural specialists within the school and parents, so they can get an understanding of why a student behaves in the way that they do, but more importantly what needs to be done to support the student. Schools can help by having very simple behavioural plans in place that take into account the school environment. Furthermore, strategies recommended for students need to be simple and achievable. I promote the idea of working on one specific behavioural change at a time. Unfortunately, too many professionals write reports and recommendations which are simply impossible to implement within a classroom and school environment due to lack of resources but also due to a lack of understanding of how classrooms work.

More professional development

The teachers I meet are crying out for more professional development in how best to manage some of the daily behavioural challenges that are faced. So many teachers feel unsupported and the majority of the day is spent managing a small number of students, while not teaching the majority of the class.

Teachers can be helped by attending workshops, having external professionals come in to watch students and advise on behavioural strategies and by working with fellow staff to develop a range of techniques and strategies to manage the behaviours of students. Being given time away from challenging students should also be considered.

Setting up mentoring and peer support for teachers should be a given in schools, particularly for teachers who have challenging classes.

In the last two years I have met a number of teachers who have been teaching for two years or less. These teachers have been referred to me for counselling assistance by their local doctor due to high levels of stress, which in turn has developed into an adjustment disorder – mixed anxiety and depression. When talking to the teachers, the following common themes appear:

- University education has not prepared them for the demands of teaching.
- There is a feeling of lack of support from senior members of staff.
- It is impossible to teach as the bulk of teaching time is spent purely on managing behaviours.
- There are little or no consequences for poor behaviours in schools.
- Too many parents blame the school/teacher.
- Too many parents expect the teacher to solve all of the behavioural issues of their child.
- Teachers are afraid to admit that they are finding things difficult for fear of looking weak and jeopardising future contract positions and employment.

It is so clear that teachers need more support in managing challenging behaviours, but also more professional development and support programmes.

More external professional support

As previously mentioned, I become concerned when I read reports from professionals who have absolutely no idea on how schools work or what a classroom environment is and how it functions. To add to this, teachers are placed under more pressure from professional reports which parents don't understand because they have not been explained within a school context. So what can schools do?

The best outcome is for schools to engage with professionals who have had experience as teachers. You would hope that then the professional knows how schools and classrooms work and can then make recommendations based on knowledge of the school and classroom environment. These professionals are out there, albeit in small quantities, but worth the search.

If this is not possible the next best option is for schools to develop a good working relationship with a range of professionals who are happy to visit the school on a regular basis to support staff and students. An ongoing working relationship allows schools to develop trust with a professional. I see it as the role of the various educational bodies to support schools by providing them with funding to access professionals of the schools' choice.

Finally, professionals need to listen to teachers. The following example highlights a clear lack of communication:

A teacher reported to me about her class where a young boy was placed on Ritalin for attention deficit hyperactivity disorder (ADHD) and the teacher and entire staff of the school were shocked. Why? Because the student was a lovely boy at school, completed his work to a good level, had friends and showed no signs of any behavioural difficulties. At home this was a completely different story which resulted in the parents going to a paediatrician who diagnosed ADHD and placed the student on medication. If the paediatrician had sought advice from the school the diagnosis would certainly have been very different.

Professionals need to talk to teachers as well as parents when making a diagnosis that impacts upon learning and behaviour at school.

Better understanding from parents

Unfortunately, we are now living in a society where many parents have the expectation that schools and teachers will basically raise their children and 'fix them'. This is not helped by professionals who fill parents' heads with ideas and, in doing so, create completely unrealistic expectations of teachers.

What we need in schools is parents who are supporting teachers, understand their own child's needs in regard to learning and behaviour and who value education. The parents I would love to see more of are ones who are willing to work with and not against the school, to achieve the best possible educational outcomes for their child.

Unfortunately, we now have parents who through their behaviours are setting their children up for failure later in life. Some common terms being bandied about for parents are gunship, lawnmower and helicopter, and these terms are used to describe parents who constantly rescue their children which in turn leads to children growing into adults who have no resilience. The children of helicopter parents are raised to never experience disappointment, fail at anything or lose. This is so far away from the real world.

CASE STUDY

The lawnmower parent (definition – the parent who clears the pathway for their child)

Jonathon is ten years old and to date his life has been one success to the next but recently his behaviour in the classroom has deteriorated. Jonathon has become very disruptive, defiant to teachers, unwilling to complete school work and at times very negative in his attitude and language towards his peers. Jonathon's teachers noticed that he appeared to be struggling in understanding some concepts in maths, but most interestingly, Jonathon was no longer the best at everything. With an intake of students in Year 5, Jonathon now had many more students in the year group who were also very good at activities.

An interview between Jonathon's mother (Mrs S) and classroom teacher deteriorated very quickly as Mrs S would not believe anything that the teacher said in regard to Jonathon's behaviours at school. Mrs S was very quick to blame the teacher for not stimulating Jonathon at school while also directing the blame for Jonathon's behaviours to other students within the classroom. Jonathon not completing work was due to it being boring. It was very clear that according to Mrs S, Jonathon was not responsible for any of his behaviours, it was everyone else who was to blame. Mrs S also was quick to point out that Jonathon had never had any difficulties before.

Background information gained from Jonathon's previous teachers revealed that Mrs S was a typical lawnmower parent. Throughout his schooling Jonathon was rescued by his mother so he never had to take any responsibility for his behaviour or actions. If Jonathon did not get a good mark Mrs S would ring the teacher and ask why, and then justify why the mark needed to be higher. If Jonathon did not get to learn the instrument he wanted to, Mrs S would ring and manoeuvre things so he could. If Jonathon did not get to be in a dormitory with his close friends on a school camp, Mrs S would ring the school. There were countless examples of Mrs S clearing the path so Jonathon could get what he wanted.

The end result was a meeting between the school principal and Mrs S. To his credit the principal asked Mrs S this question: 'What does success look like for Jonathon when he leaves our school?' This question stumped Mrs S somewhat, before replying that in her view success was winning academic awards, being good at sport and music, with the ultimate success being in winning a scholarship to a prestigious school. Mrs S went on to say that it was her job to make this happen. To this the principal responded with 'What happens if it doesn't? What will happen to Jonathon?' Unfortunately Mrs S could not rationalise this, despite the principal's best efforts to convince Mrs S that the goal was for Jonathon to achieve success but also for Jonathon to learn how to both win and lose. You don't always get everything you want in life and sometimes it is the disappointments that we experience that motivate us to achieve.

Mrs S withdrew Jonathon from the school four weeks later as she was no longer getting what she wanted as Jonathon's teacher was not caving in to her demands and was being supported by the principal in her actions.

I am seeing more and more lawnmower parents and the pressure they place on their children is enormous. I often have children referred to me with illness, anxiety and sometimes depression and the primary cause is that the child cannot meet the expectation of the parents, despite the parents clearing the way.

What we need is to educate parents on the challenges their child faces as a result of the behaviours displayed. We need to have resources available both internally and externally for parents to access and, most importantly, parents who are supporting the teachers and schools. Parent seminars and forums at the start of the year are a great way to communicate expectations and lay the ground rules for parents in regard to communication with teachers and schools.

We also need an understanding from parents of students who are in classes with students who have challenging behaviours. Class harmony and teacher stress levels are severely impacted by demanding parents who cannot see the bigger picture and understand that schools and teachers are trying to teach and support all children and not just their own.

Informed, involved and realistic parents are the goal.

Better understanding from fellow staff

Getting staff on board to support students with challenging behaviours is a challenge for most schools. Unfortunately, in many of the schools I visit I see what would be called 'old-school teachers' who believe teaching should be as it was in the 1950s and 1960s and who, as a result, have very little tolerance for students with challenging behaviours. This can also make life challenging for younger teachers who are often asked to teach the challenging students because the unsupporting teachers won't (as they are made to feel inadequate and believe that they have done their time in challenging classrooms).

As a part of my work I visit schools and work with recent graduate teachers. A common thread is that the teachers do not want to admit they are finding managing a class difficult, but also that they often feel unsupported by colleagues and, in some cases, the leadership team. Recently I have provided counselling services to teachers in a rural town in South Australia where there are many social problems and, as a result, many students with challenging behaviours in schools. A consistent thought of teachers was that the leadership team of the school did not support them and in one case a teacher was told, 'I coped in the class for five years, why can't you?'

The sad fact is that the leadership teams are doing everything they can to manage behaviour, deal with parents, meet curriculum demands etc. and are often struggling themselves.

So what do we need to do?

Staff need to develop a culture unique to their school. What does this entail? Basically it is up to a school to create a set of rules and guidelines that the entire school community will follow. Sporting clubs, businesses and community groups alike do this. We see values and goal statements in so many places we visit and we need schools to get on board with the staff, all committing to living the values.

In a school I recently visited which had many students with challenging behaviours, the principal has worked hard at creating a new culture based around respect for learning, the environment we learn in, and each other. It has taken time for all of the teachers to embrace the culture, but now I see classrooms where students sit, stand, lie, kneel or even walk when learning and, guess what, the students love it. I see a room where there are fun, challenging, hands-on learning activities that students want to visit. I see consequences which are meaningful, but most importantly, I see a staff who fully support each other and are willing to help students with behavioural needs.

A big shift has also been in the behaviour of staff in the staffroom. All negative talk about students has been banned from the room. Positive events are noted on a board for everyone to see. Staff actively seek out children and congratulate them on an achievement. In a nutshell we have staff that are positive and encouraging and the outcome is an increase of well-being for all, increased learning outcomes, and a significant reduction in the challenging behaviours of children.

How to develop a staff culture

Many organisations take a lot of time to develop a staff culture and inevitably it fails to be implemented due to the staff not buying into the values and plans of the culture. Unfortunately, schools are too often no different. Why is this?

The answer is simple. In some schools there are teachers who are very set in their ways and unwilling to make changes. I am sure you can identify them in your school setting. My thoughts on this are very clear: do not let a minority stop the majority making a positive difference. My other observation in schools is that when positive changes are made, staff generally will follow but it does take some longer than others!

So how do schools develop a positive culture? The critical factor is to keep it very simple and achievable for all. I encourage schools to establish a set of very easy-to-follow rules (as we do for students) for staff. These can start by agreeing that all staff will call students by their names. If a staff member doesn't know a name they simply ask the student what their name is before beginning the conversation. The same process is followed with parents. Name tags are used.

The second step is to identify some behaviours that staff need to change to create a positive culture. This might be arriving to class on time or always having lunch in the staffroom. Little behaviours from staff help to create a positive school culture.

Thirdly, I encourage staff to create traditions such as celebrating birthdays, having regular social occasions, playing other schools in sports or games, or simply using some staff meeting time to have fun as a group and share information.

24

The creation of a positive culture does not need to be complex. It is about creating a set of easy rules for all staff to follow. Three or four per term to work on is enough, as over the year the school will become a very positive place to be. Remember, staff can drive this if they have the motivation and opportunity.

Whole-school approach to managing behaviours

As previously mentioned, developing a staff culture that supports students with challenging behaviours is a big starting point and this then needs to be followed by creating a school community that supports all of the students within it. Fortunately, if the staff create the culture, the community is likely to follow.

To get a school community involved, the following strategies can be applied:

- Provide education and training for parents.
- Encourage all members of the school community into the school.
- Bring in the expertise of parents where possible to help educate staff and fellow parents on topics, but specifically, challenging behaviours.
- Staff need to attend school functions and meet parents.
- Schools need to make the environment inviting for members of the school community. Simple things such as having signs with directions help enormously.
- Communicate to parents and the community via the internet and school newsletters.
- Encourage people within the community to volunteer to help in classrooms with learning or mentoring for children who have challenging behaviours.

A school where the teachers' well-being is considered

I recently attended an end-of-year school celebration and I was surprised to see two parents attending who I knew were both teachers at the same school. My initial question was: 'How did you get the day off to attend?' I was very pleased to hear that the school offers all of the staff four days per year that can be taken for special occasions such as celebration days, sports days, moving days or appointments. This made me think of how important it is to support the well-being of the teachers and staff of a school. I believe that any organisation is only going to be as good as its greatest asset, and in schools the greatest asset is the teaching staff. It needs to be well looked after.

Many schools are starting to introduce well-being programmes for staff; however, progress is sometimes slow. Some of the barriers to effective well-being programmes are:

- Lack of money to support staff well-being programmes.
- Staff perception that well-being is not important but students' results are.
- School boards and management not valuing the well-being of staff.
- Large class sizes with more and more students with high needs.
- Greater demands being placed on teacher time.
- Teachers being scared to ask for help or support.
- Teachers putting their students and jobs before themselves, resulting in low levels of well-being.

Schools can introduce a variety of programmes to support staff. In doing so, educational outcomes will improve for the students because we will have the majority of teachers are coming to work happy and feeling good about themselves and their whole working environment.

In a perfect world all of these things would be happening, but we all know this does not exist. The challenge that lies ahead for schools is to try to implement some of the suggested changes so students are free to learn without distraction and students with challenging behaviours are accepted and catered for where possible within the classroom and school.

So now I hope you are thinking of the perfect school and teaching environment and what needs to be done to create this. To work towards creating this perfect environment we need to ask the question of why. That is, why are there now so many more challenging behaviours presenting? The next two chapters will look at the types of behaviours that present and also the cause of the behaviours.

 # What are challenging behaviours?

I recently asked a group of teachers to come up with as many challenging behaviours as they could in 15 minutes. The list is below and very comprehensive.

- Shyness
- Rocking
- Staring
- Anxiety
- School phobia
- Constantly distracted
- Truancy
- Social isolation
- Hand flapping
- Being out of seat
- Calling out in class
- Tantrums
- Swearing
- Screaming
- Refusing to follow instructions
- Work avoidance
- Arriving late
- Persistent breaking of class rules
- Verbal abuse of other pupils
- General 'mucking about'
- Physical aggression to other pupils
- Verbal abuse to teacher
- Not getting on with work
- Head banging
- Poor body language
- Kicking
- Biting
- Punching
- Fighting
- Running away
- Smashing equipment or furniture/fixtures
- Physical destructiveness
- Physical aggression to teacher
- Inappropriate conversations
- Depression
- Self-harm
- Fiddling
- Destroying own work
- Not sitting still
- Not listening
- Stealing
- Stubbornness
- Disrupting games of others
- Making noises randomly
- Obsessions
- Being over-affectionate
- Inappropriate touching

As you can see there are many facets to managing behaviour in a school due to the enormous variety in behaviour that occurs. I believe the best thing we can do as teachers is to work towards understanding the cause of any behaviour, because once we know why a student behaves in a certain way we can work towards creating the calm environment that best supports the student's individual learning needs. Now let us look more specifically at the causes of the challenging behaviours.

5 | What are the causes of challenging behaviours in students?

When observing or working with any student, the first question I always ask myself is 'Why?' What is the cause of the behaviours? Having thought about this a lot and having worked with and listened to students and parents alike, I have decided that most behaviours are caused by one or more of the following:

1 Overall level of intelligence.
2 Ability to access the curriculum.
3 Undiagnosed or diagnosed medical condition.
4 The environment that a child lives in and the impact upon the social, emotional and learning development of the child.
5 A student making the choice to behave in a way that allows them to meet their immediate needs.
6 The quality of the relationship between student and teacher.

Teachers and staff need to understand what combination of the above is causing the classroom behaviours, so then strategies to manage the behaviour can be developed. I will describe each of the areas in more detail.

Overall level of intelligence

When working with students who have challenging behaviours, the first question I always ask is 'What is the cause?' The second question is generally 'What is the overall cognitive ability of the student?' That is, does the student have the intelligence or brain functioning power to understand their behaviours, the consequences of their behaviours, the strategies being put in place to help them and, most importantly, have the ability to change their behaviours?

We must not forget that students of all intelligence levels display challenging behaviours and this is why I strongly encourage students who show consistent challenging behaviours to have an evaluation/ assessment by an external professional, so then teachers, parents and sometimes the student can understand how a student thinks and why they behave in the manner they do. One of the evaluation tools is an assessment of overall cognitive ability or intelligence test.

A quick lesson in how I measure intelligence. As a psychologist I use a test called a Wechsler Intelligence Scale (WISC), and this is the most widely used test around the world for children aged between 6 and 16. The WISC provides an overall intelligence score with ranges and percentiles. The ranges and percentiles look like this:

Extremely High – above the 98th percentile.
Very High – between the 90th and 98th percentile.
High Average – between the 75th and 90th percentile.
Average – between the 25th and 75th percentile.
Low Average – between the 9th and 25th percentile.
Borderline – between the 2nd and 9th percentile.
Extremely Low – below the 2nd percentile.

From here the WISC can be broken down into five scales:

Verbal Comprehension – measures verbal reasoning and acquired verbal knowledge.

Visual Spatial – measures a student's visual-spatial processing, understanding of part-whole relationships and visual-motor integration.

Fluid Reasoning – measures a student's logical reasoning, conceptual thinking, broad visual intelligence and classification abilities.

Working Memory – measures a student's visual and visual-spatial short-term memory, as well as selective attention and concentration.

Processing Speed – measures a student's perceptual speed, rate of task completion, visual scanning/tracking and discrimination of simple visual information.

It is from the breakdown of the scales and observation during the assessment that I learn a lot about a student and possibly why they behave in the manner that they do.

CASE STUDY

James is 16 years old and in Year 11 at school. James was assessed to be in the Superior range of intelligence at age six and he has always found school easy, obtaining high marks with very little effort. James has chosen to study specialist maths, physics, chemistry, economics and information processing, as he loves playing on and working with computers.

Recently, James has become more and more disengaged at school and at home. His teachers have contacted his parents raising concerns that James is often not attending classes, feels sick during lessons and does not complete or hand in work. James had also been asked to leave the class on a number of occasions due to being rude to teachers and for being disruptive. At home, James is spending a large amount of time in his room playing on the computer and he is very hard to get out of bed in the morning.

James was reassessed with his overall score placing him in the High Average range. James had scores in the Extremely High range for Verbal Comprehension, Fluid Reasoning and Visual Spatial with his score in the Working Memory area placing him in the High Average range. Of note was that James's score in the Processing Speed range was in the Average range and at the 45th percentile which indicates that when compared to his scores in the other areas, James has a weakness with his Processing Speed.

James was open and honest when we met and he indicated that he had no idea what he wanted to do with his life and he was only doing his chosen subjects because his parents and teachers said he should. James also admitted to spending too much time on the computer and that he did not do any homework. The last thing that James explained was that he found the work difficult this year as there was so much more of it.

Why was James behaving as he was? What was the cause?

James did not have the skills to be able to study at home as he had always found his work easy and never had to do homework. James was finding keeping up with the work difficult due to his processing speed. He was spending too much time playing games on the computer and he was scared about what the future held for him.

Old-school psychology taught me about the flight or fight response. James had chosen the flight response and he was being disruptive, withdrawing and absorbing himself in the computer to hide from the fact he was finding school challenging.

The solutions for James are included as Appendix 1. Have an attempt at writing down five solutions and see how they compare to my approach.

Some of the questions I ask in classrooms are:

- Is a student being disruptive because they don't know what to do in class? A poor working memory would mean that a student is not retaining the instructions.
- Is a student having social problems because they don't process the verbal information (working memory), have difficulty in communicating (low verbal comprehension skills) and difficulty in reading body language (low visual spatial skills)?
- Is a student having temper tantrums, outbursts, displays of violence, but not understanding consequences or the strategies to help (low overall ability)?

The combinations are endless, but it is what can be learned about the cause of behaviour through intelligence on which I focus. I understand that teachers and schools simply do not have the time or resources to assess every student, but what we can look at is past school reports, standardised testing results and general day-to-day work output when compared to peers. It is this information that may give us some clues. Special education or learning needs teachers are also a very useful source of information.

One of my (preferred) approaches when working with older students who are showing challenging behaviours is to make school easier for them and 'put a light at the end of the tunnel for them'. This means using an assessment to identify learning strengths and weaknesses, identify career interests, and then work out to what subjects a student is best suited, so they can progress through school. For a 14-year-old to hear, 'It is okay to find maths, science and English hard, but you need to have a go, but I want you to do well in art, tech, PE and music because that is where your strengths are', is very reassuring. I also talk to schools about modifying subjects and creating pathways for students as this helps students to see the future and assists in changing behavioural attitudes to school.

A note for teachers: When writing reports and stating that a student is not organised, always ask why and what can I do to help them become better organised? An example I have used for a student in Year 3 was to only have one book for school and one for home. This way the student only had to look after one book at school and was not forever looking for books. It also saved paper! Does the student need visual reminders, regular checks on diary notes, work progress etc.? Teachers need to teach students how to be organised and not just assume it happens naturally.

When managing challenging behaviours, I want teachers to ask 'Why?' If we can find the answer, it makes putting strategies into place to manage the behaviour much easier.

Ability to access the curriculum

The ability of a student to access the curriculum can be obtained through a cognitive assessment; however, it is how we modify the curriculum to allow students to access the curriculum that matters. Unfortunately, our curriculum has become so overloaded it has become much harder for teachers to adjust the curriculum to meet the needs of the entire class and, as a result, disruptive behaviour occurs.

What I have observed is very much a fight or flight response from students who can't access the curriculum. On one hand, we have the fight response and this manifests itself in behaviours such as defiance, calling out, wandering around the room, disrupting others and generally not completing school work. On the other hand, we have the flight response and this is where students will forget work, not bring materials to school, not complete assignments or homework tasks, be absent from lessons due to illness, be late to classes or be very quiet in the classroom so as not to draw any attention to themselves.

CASE STUDY

A 12-year-old girl, Sophie, was referred for an assessment as she had transferred into a new middle school which completed standardised testing as a part of the enrolment process. The middle school teachers had noticed that Sophie had difficulty keeping up with the workload, took much longer than her peers to complete tasks and that her test results were well below the average for the class. It was also noted that Sophie was missing some classes due to attending the school counsellor or being in the sick room.

Sophie's parents indicated that she was a delightful girl who always worked hard on her homework and who was very popular at school, but recently she had started to be sick a lot in the morning and that she had become very defensive, if not secretive, about her school studies. At school, Sophie was very quiet and she always achieved results that were okay.

Sophie completed an assessment and it was discovered that she was Dyslexic. When asked how she had done so well through primary school, Sophie provided the following explanations:

- I had very good friends from whom I could copy work.
- I would spend a lot of time doing homework.
- I only had one teacher so I could talk to the teacher and distract them from my work.
- My work was always very neat and well presented.
- I was very quiet at school, never drawing any attention to myself.

Sophie had developed great survival skills in the classroom but in a middle school environment with lots of teachers and a higher work expectation, Sophie was beginning to struggle. What came with her struggle was the fight or flight response and in this case it was the flight response that was starting to present.

Fortunately for Sophie, her struggle to access the curriculum was recognised and what was expected of her from a work point of view was modified. Sophie ceased studying a second language and the free lessons were used for learning support. Communication was also established between Sophie, her parents and teachers so Sophie could communicate when she was experiencing difficulty, resulting in modifications being made to the curriculum where necessary. Sophie was able to regain her enthusiasm for learning.

Being able to access the curriculum is so important for students in regard to their behaviour at school. As teachers we must also remember that sometimes students may not like a subject and that this is okay. We all have areas of interest, areas in which we excel and areas in which we do not excel. As teachers we must not take it personally if a student does not like our subject or what is being taught. The challenge sometimes is to modify the curriculum to make it more engaging for students.

I have observed that it is often when students move into a middle school or high school setting that behaviour deteriorates and it is very often due to not being able to access the curriculum. In primary school a teacher gets to know a student very well and modifications are made easily. Unfortunately, in high school it is much harder for teachers to modify due to the educational and vocational pathway requirements. However, the important factor to remember is that in order to manage behaviour we need students to have an enthusiasm for learning, a healthy self-esteem and a good working relationship with their teachers. Being able to access the curriculum while achieving some success at school goes a long way to making these three things happen!

Undiagnosed or diagnosed medical condition

For many teachers, sometimes it is glaringly obvious that a student has a condition that causes them to behave in the manner that they do. In some cases this is diagnosed by an external professional and in many cases teachers, through training, experience and observation, have worked it out for themselves. It is not up to teachers to make a diagnosis, but I think it is very important that teachers observe, record and present factual information to parents about behaviour so parents can then look to get a diagnosis or seek support. The important thing is understanding the condition, so teachers can then apply appropriate behavioural strategies.

With knowledge and greater research there are now so many more conditions that present in classrooms every day. Some of the more common conditions are:

- Attention deficit hyperactivity disorder (ADHD).
- Autism spectrum disorder (ASD).
- Oppositional defiance disorder (ODD).
- Specific learning disability (SLD).
- Impulse control disorder (ICD).
- Internet gaming disorder (IGD).

This is what I look for as cues to the above:

ADHD – can't sit still, constantly fiddles, always moving, when sitting at desk always stopping and looking around at sounds, out of the window or any distraction, poor work output.

Autism spectrum disorder – no eye contact, poor social interactions, alone at break or lunch, obsessive about items, poor motor skills.

Oppositional defiance disorder – does not follow instructions, does what they want and not what they are asked to do, argues with teachers, stubborn, likes to dictate play, happy when things going their way.

Specific learning disability – poor motor coordination, difficulty understanding instructions, poor work output, slow progress in literacy and numeracy.

Impulse control disorder – makes poor decisions, doesn't understand consequences relating to actions, reacts without thinking of what is happening and the subsequent actions.

Internet gaming disorder – appears tired, withdrawing from peers and social interactions, stops physical exercise, stops completing school work, acts out what is on screen.

Of course, there are many others that appear such as explosive intermittent disorder, generalised anxiety disorder, depression, reactive attachment disorder; however it is the ones I have described above that I tend to see the most in classrooms.

When a teacher has concerns about a student and there is no formal diagnosis, I recommend that data of behaviour is collected. In collecting data about a student I encourage teachers to keep records that look at frequency of behaviours, time when it occurs, precursors, duration of behaviour and what leads to reduction of the behaviour.

Once data has been collected, checklists pertaining to a specific diagnosis can be completed. While not providing a diagnosis, they can act as a guide and be passed on to the professional to assist in the diagnostic process. As previously mentioned, this process would stop children who only have ADHD at home and not at school being placed on medication, or at least I hope it would.

Appendix 3 gives specific strategies I recommend for teachers for all of the above conditions, but please use the checklists as a guide and not a diagnostic tool. The checklists are used to learn more about a student.

Again, staff training is very important in this process and also in helping teachers communicate the information to parents. Many parents do not react well to having it suggested that their child has a condition which is causing them to behave as they do, so careful consideration has to be given as to how the information is presented to parents. The language used when talking to parents has to be considered based on what is known of them. I recommend that the most important thing that is stressed in the meeting is that, as teachers, we want the best for your child in regard to their education and well-being.

CASE STUDY

I recently worked with a student named Dylan who was eight years old and displayed the following behaviours:

- Lacked motor skills – fell over during a dance lesson due to tangling feet.
- Did not understand personal space.
- Made no eye contact when talking.
- Refused to do school work if he didn't like it.
- Ran out of the classroom when stressed.
- Stared into space for long periods.

What was also noticeable was that Dylan was dirty, that his school uniform was dirty and he smelled unpleasant. Dylan also looked very thin and malnourished. Staff reported that he lived alone with his father on a farm and he spent a large amount of time alone. Staff also disclosed that the father was somewhat unsociable within the community and he did not see that Dylan had any problems at all and he was simply a normal boy. Notifications of neglect had been made to the relevant organisations; however, the organisations had not followed up as the case was seen as a low priority.

Staff had completed data collection and checklists; however, the father dismissed them. It was suggested that the father and Dylan attend some family counselling, but again the father dismissed this idea saying, 'I was just the same as Dylan when I was his age and I am fine now'. Unfortunately, this was not the case as Dylan was lacking in overall care, social and emotional development. What do we do?

A meeting was organised between myself and the father as it was hypothesised that the father had only ever had dealings with female staff and female external professionals (speech and psychology at kindergarten) and that maybe talking to a male would help to get the message across to him about helping to improve his parenting. Unfortunately, the father did not attend, just failed to show up. The message was very clear that the father did not want any outside interventions. All we could now do was to slowly put strategies into place to help Dylan.

What did we do to help Dylan? The answers are included as Appendix 4. But have a go first and write down five ideas of things you could try.

The key to looking at a diagnosed condition that causes challenging behaviour is whether a child can control the behaviour, as in most cases the child cannot. Where this differs from intelligence level is that many students with a diagnosed condition have very good overall levels of cognitive ability and they are very capable of completing the required school work, but their condition leads to behaviours which stop this from happening.

The important thing for schools and teachers is to learn to understand the condition and how it impacts upon the behaviour of the student. Once this happens, modifications and strategies can be put into place to support the student.

The student's home environment

One of the biggest frustrations that teachers report to me is the fact that they have no control over the environment that students live in and how this environment impacts upon their day-to-day behaviours at school. The reality is the environment that a student lives in has a huge impact upon their day-to-day behaviour.

Some of the factors that heavily influence behaviours of students are:

1 **Sleep**. If a student comes to school tired they lack the ability to concentrate, but also rationalise their decisions. A high proportion of poor behaviour can be attributed to children not getting enough sleep.

2 **Diet**. Teachers receive students in the morning who are loaded up on sugar and not able to concentrate, or conversely, students who have had no food and are lethargic as a result.

3 **Role modelling of parents**. If parents role model good behaviours, children will follow. It is hard to manage students who see behaviours at home which are not acceptable at school. This causes confusion for young students.

4 **Separated parents.** Many students are smart and will play their parents off against each other leading to students always getting what they want. This, in turn, can lead to poor behaviours at school. The classic one I see is where one parent has no rules at home, so children go to bed when they want, eat what they want and do what they want. This leads to poor choices, which impacts upon behaviours at school.

5 **Too much TV and screen time.** It is evident that we have more and more students who spend so much time playing games that addictions occur, which impacts upon behaviours at school. I mentioned Internet Gaming Disorder which is a relatively new diagnosis, but growing rapidly.

6 **Pushy parents or high expectation parents.** Students who have parents with very high expectations can exhibit challenging behaviours, particularly when they are struggling to meet the expectations. Teachers see disruptive and avoidance behaviours.

7 **Environments where the word NO does not exist.** I am seeing more and more of what I call 'peerents' not parents. A peerent wants to be friends with their child and not a parent who sets rules and boundaries. Peerented children often display challenging behaviours as they cannot cope with the word 'no'.

CASE STUDY

Andrew presents as a 13-year-old boy who is not happy at school, tired, lacking in motivation, not completing school work and generally moody and unhappy. Andrew's mother reported that Andrew enjoys playing basketball but he has lost motivation to go to practice and it has become a battle to get him to the games. However, when he is there, he enjoys spending the time with his friends. It was noted that Andrew is spending more and more time on his computer. Andrew's mother believes that he has depression.

When talking, Andrew reveals that he is spending a lot of time on the computer talking to his friends, but when questioned further, Andrew explains that his computer friends live in the United Kingdom and America.

When thinking about this it occurred to me that there is a very big time difference between where Andrew is in Australia, and America and the United Kingdom. What was happening was that Andrew was staying up very late at night talking to his friends on Skype and as a result not getting very much sleep. The result of this was a tired, moody, unmotivated Andrew.

The immediate solution was to monitor Andrew's time on the computer and restrict his access in the evening so he would go to bed; however, Andrew's mother was very reluctant to do this as this would cause conflict between herself and Andrew. This is a very typical example of so many households today and as a result I am seeing so many clients like Andrew who are living their lives through the computer.

The solutions were to talk to Andrew about his friendships online, his school work, friends outside of school, and hobbies other than the computer and to help him to develop a much better balance. Support was also going to be needed for Andrew's mother so she could implement some changes at home that would help Andrew to go to bed earlier but also to re-establish his friendships.

This is not designed to be a parenting book; however, I believe it can be seen that the environment in which children live can have a huge impact upon their day-to-day behaviour. What we need are parents who value education and will support teachers by setting up good stable home environments for their children, so they come to school ready and willing to learn.

The choice of the student

Another cause of challenging behaviour at school is simply the choice of the student. I find that some students have what I call 'look at me' syndrome (LAM) and, as a result, challenging behaviours occur.

Is it that a student wants to impress their peers to be accepted into a group and as a result teachers see challenging behaviours in class? Or is it that a student thinks this teacher has no control so 'I will see what I can get away with to impress my peers'?

Students can also choose to behave poorly to be removed from classes they simply don't like. I have met students who do not like a teacher, so they do everything they can to be excluded from the class. In all other classes they behave appropriately.

Finally, and I find this quite extraordinary, I met a small group of students who chose to behave poorly so they could get a Friday detention (stay in until 5 pm on Friday after school). The reasoning was that the students loved the elderly lady who always supervised the detention class. She told stories, listened to the students, helped them with homework and made the time fun. A student described this to me as his favourite class of the week, yet it was driving his parents to despair as he was always getting in trouble at school, albeit for minor things.

We mustn't forget that sometime students will simply choose to behave in a challenging manner to enable their needs to be met.

To understand challenging behaviours we must know the cause because once we know and understand the cause, we are on the path to creating and putting into place strategies to help manage the behaviour.

The quality of the relationship between the teacher and student

I encourage you to think back to your own schooling. Who were the good teachers? Why were they the good teachers? What were the qualities of the teacher that made them good?

I cannot remember who taught me 'i before e except after c', how to do my seven times table, the first 20 elements of the periodic table or how to play table tennis, but I remember vividly the teachers who took an interest in me as a person, encouraged me to have a go and made learning fun. Most importantly they created an enthusiasm for learning so I would wake up each day and want to go to school. Here is my favourite school memory.

My favourite school memory is from Year 6 of primary school. I had a teacher named Mr Yates who was an elderly man, fairly firm in his rules and expectations. However, he also had a great sense of humour and a love of English literature, reading to us nearly every day from some great literary work. Mr Yates also loved the game of chess and he was willing to give up his lunch and break times to teach anyone who wanted to learn how to play. I wanted to learn and I did learn, very quickly.

Mr Yates would be playing against four or five students at once and he quickly realised that I had a natural talent for the game. This led to more one-on-one battles during lesson times (in the afternoons once I had finished all of my work) and my game rapidly improved. I continued to play in my high school years, winning my school championship as a Year 8 student and spending many years as the number one player in the school.

This was an amazing schooltime experience, but had even better long-term ramifications. The school to which I was applying for my first job post-university wanted a Registered Teacher who could teach PE but also who could teach and run a chess programme. I won the position. I will never forget Mr Yates because he taught me how to play chess, which played an integral part in helping me to obtain my first teaching appointment.

What point does this story reinforce? It is how important the teacher–student relationship is in learning but in also managing student behaviour. I struggled with my learning but because Mr Yates took an interest in me and spent time teaching me something I loved, I worked harder and my behaviour was good in class. I developed an enthusiasm for learning and school.

When students respect and have good relationships with their teachers, problematic behaviours are reduced significantly. Students listen to the teachers they have a good relationship with and are more likely to try to improve challenging behaviours because they understand that someone cares about them. I see this daily in my visits to schools. How often in your school will a student only go to a certain teacher to talk to and calm down? What is it about that teacher?

I have asked many students over the past years what it is about their teachers that have helped them to manage their behaviour and feel good about going to school. Here are some of their thoughts:

- The teacher knows my name.
- The teacher knows I love football.
- The teacher likes *The Simpsons*.
- The teacher has a cool room with crazy toys and puzzles.
- The teacher doesn't tell me what to do all of the time.
- The teacher listens to me.
- The teacher has time to help me when I am angry.
- The teacher helps me with my school work.
- The teacher tells funny stories and jokes.

- The teacher plays with me in the yard when on duty.
- The teacher always says good things about my school work.
- The teacher has taught me what to do when I am angry.
- The teacher makes learning fun.
- The teacher gives me work I can do.
- The teacher takes us outside to learn when the weather is good.
- The teacher tells the class about themselves and how they are feeling.

All of the above contribute to developing good relationships between students and teachers. This leads to better behaviour from students because they feel valued and a part of the learning process.

CASE STUDY

Amy is six years old and in Year 2 at school. She has been diagnosed as having global developmental delay, ASD, a very low adaptive functioning level, severe language delay and severe sensory processing disorder. Amy is in a classroom with 24 other students and she has one-to-one support in the classroom for 23 hours per week.

Amy lives at home with her mother and two younger siblings. Amy rarely sees her father as her parents separated when she was four years old. Amy's mother indicated that she finds it very hard to manage Amy at home and the use of an iPad is the best way to keep Amy calm. Amy is receiving speech therapy and occupational therapy while her mother is working with a counsellor to support her family.

The following behaviours were observed of Amy in the classroom: Amy cannot access the curriculum. Amy is happy when she is working on an iPad. She becomes violent when she does not get her way and she will hit, kick, yell, scream and throw objects when angry. Amy tries to interact with her peers but finds it hard to communicate with them. Amy gets up and walks around the room at random. She likes to walk around outside of the classroom. Amy needs help to go to the toilet. She struggles with her fine and gross motor skills.

Amy's teacher explained that without one-to-one support, she cannot manage Amy in the classroom as often Amy is violent with her peers or she will yell and scream when not getting her way. Many of the class are scared of Amy due to her violent reactions.

The first question that needs to be addressed is whether the school is the best one for Amy. This appears to be very harsh, but given Amy's level of need it is necessary to determine if Amy would be better suited to being in a school that is better able to meet her needs and provide an educational structure that will help her to learn to settle better into the routines and learning of school.

In order for Amy to move to a school that will cater better to her needs, a school must be available and have a place for her. Unfortunately, in many remote or rural locations schools for students with high needs do not exist. Furthermore, in many cities and towns, there are no available student places due to high demand. When this occurs, schools are forced to adapt and this is where the challenges lie. So how can schools adapt?

In Amy's case the following strategies were put into place in agreement with her mother: Amy was in the classroom until lunchtime on Tuesday, Wednesday and Thursday with full days on Monday and Friday. On Tuesday, Wednesday and Thursday Amy was withdrawn from class to attend appointments such as speech therapy and occupational therapy. Amy also attended a social skills training programme when not in class, which was conducted by the school counsellor.

The focus was on working on one behaviour change at a time and the first focus was to remove the violent reactions. This was done through teaching Amy strategies to calm herself. Hand signals, anger colour cards and a chart with face expressions were used so Amy could show her support person when she was angry.

Amy was given a safe place in the classroom where she could sit when feeling angry. She was provided with cues to help her to stop hitting people such as wearing a band aid on her finger. Amy was able to use her iPad at all times to complete learning tasks. Amy was supported with her play by staff at break and lunchtimes. She was provided with lots of positive reinforcement by the entire school community and she was given tasks which were of benefit to the school.

The management of every student who has challenging behaviours will be unique, based upon the needs of the student, the resources available within a school, the support of parents but also and most importantly the safety of staff and students. In Amy's case the school were able to support her and in time Amy developed more positive behaviours, but her learning progress was very slow.

It is hard to determine what was going to be best for Amy in regard to her schooling and this is where lots of open and honest communication is needed. More importantly, schools need to have the capacity to help students like Amy, whether that be in a school specifically designed for students with challenging behaviours and high levels of individual need or within the local school.

It is evident that there are many reasons why students display challenging behaviours and before we commence any form of intervention it is important that we understand the cause. If the cause is unknown, intervention becomes much harder and, on occasions, misguided intervention can lead to an increase in challenging behaviours.

In the next chapter we will look at some practical classroom strategies that can be easily applied in a school and classroom setting, but please remember, understand the cause of the behaviour before actioning an intervention.

6 | Practical classroom strategies

Following are some suggestions to try. Different classes will require different approaches as not all strategies will work in all situations. The best piece of advice I can give to any teacher or school is to have a go and work on one behaviour at a time – I find that if we try to change too many behaviours at once, students get confused. Focus on one behaviour, create the change, cement the change, provide lots of praise and encouragement and then look to work on the next behaviour.

I find that too often teachers are scared to attempt a new strategy. If in doubt, talk to school leaders and create a plan, implement the plan and then evaluate the outcome, but please do not be afraid to try.

Strategies to manage behaviours

I have tried to put these strategies into an order with the view of prevention where possible. I have also divided the strategies into two sections: the first looking at a whole-school approach to managing behaviour and the second, more specific classroom/teaching approaches. It must be noted that many of the approaches work together and can be applied in both areas, and the best outcome is generally when this is the case. In Appendix 3, I have included some specific tips teachers can use to manage a number of behaviours including anger, defiance and lack of engagement.

Whole-school approaches to managing challenging behaviours

The following strategies work best when the entire school staff and community are all working together and supportive of positive behavioural change.

Communication between staff and parents. What do we know already and what has helped in the past?

I believe strongly in prevention and the provision of information from parents to school and from staff to staff can be so useful in planning for prevention. Unfortunately, I often meet teachers and school leaders who are given no information about a student and in many cases it is a student who has been moved from school to school due to challenging behaviours.

Some parents do not want to disclose information to schools as they either don't believe what they are being told and blame the previous school for not catering for their child's needs, or feel that the child is not at fault but rather it is everyone else who causes the behaviour. The sad thing here is that it is the child who loses out when parents are in denial. I know schools complete enrolment forms, but I want to know the following from parents:

- Why are you enrolling your child in this school?
- Does your child have a diagnosed condition that impacts upon their behaviour in the classroom?
- Are any external professionals involved in supporting your child? If so, are you happy for us to establish contact with them?
- Why did you choose to leave your last school?
- What are your expectations of this school and its teachers?
- What strategies work best to support the behaviour of your child at school?

After the answers are established I think it is important for the school to be clear about what is within its capacity to support a particular student. I have recently visited a school that has established a superb learning/ behavioural support structure from junior primary all the way to the final year of senior school. As a result, the school has attracted many students who have behavioural needs and this, in turn, has led to staff being stretched and a reduction in support for students. I know schools can't say no to students, but because of this I encourage schools to be very clear about what levels of support can be provided, so parents can then make an informed decision about what is best for their child.

The next stage is to talk to the teacher, so early intervention strategies can be put into place. I also strongly recommend that the child visits the classroom in advance, whether this be after school or at lunch or break time, so the child can learn where everything is in the new environment. The child can also meet the teacher, see where they will sit, where the toilets are, play areas etc. These are normal transition routines, but with extra emphasis towards meeting the needs of the child based on the information provided.

Teachers can also share information about a student if they are moving up a year level within a school. As a teacher I must admit I did not want to know too much about my new students, thinking I would prefer to work it out for myself when they arrive in my class. However, in some cases this cannot simply happen. I encourage teachers to have an open mind about all of their students, but to take the time to read the files of each student to be better prepared. If there are concerns raised from reading files, teachers can then go and talk to previous teachers or school leaders to gain more information. This is where new teachers to a school need support.

In middle and senior schools it is not realistically possible for teachers to read the files of every student. This is where students who have diagnosed conditions or behavioural/learning needs can be flagged in advance so teachers can then prepare to modify or set up structures to support the student. This is more work for the teacher, but I think it is worthwhile in the long term.

CASE STUDY

I worked with a student who had been diagnosed with global developmental delay (very low level of intellectual functioning) in helping to settle the student into school. The student's name was Chris and he was six years old.

To help Chris, the school and I worked on setting up an induction programme where he initially only attended school in the morning, three days per week. During this time Chris was provided with a classroom buddy and a peer buddy (Year 6 student for break) to help him understand what was happening. We also taught Chris how to use his iPad, and uploaded photos of his teachers and his classroom, so if he was lost he could show someone his iPad photos and they could direct him to where he needed to be.

Gradually the time spent at school increased and by the end of the first semester Chris was at school on a full-time basis. This was a scenario where Chris's parents provided information, supported the school and worked with Chris so he could settle into school. Parents with realistic expectations make life so much easier in schools.

Contrary to this, I have worked with a student who was simply not ready to be at school. The boy's name was Tony and he would run out of the classroom and hide at random. This created all kinds of problems for the school staff due to duty of care and safety for Tony, and increased stress levels for the staff. Even when withdrawn from class and receiving one-to-one support, Tony would run at random. The solution implemented by the school was that Tony's parents had to come and pick him up and take him home as the school did not have the resources to ensure that Tony was safe.

Slowly we worked with Tony, providing a structured reward system at school using computer games as a reward. After 18 months, Tony stopped running. We then had to sort out classroom behaviour! Why did Tony behave as he did? A mixture of ADHD, impulse control disorder, specific learning disability, lack of sleep, poor diet and too much screen time contributed to his behaviour – this probably sounds very familiar to so many teachers. Unfortunately, Tony's parents did not help by supporting the school in its work with their son but, despite this, a high level of success was achieved.

The point is schools can prepare by getting information from parents which is passed onto staff, setting up classroom structures based on the information, coordinating support time, establishing lines of communication with parents and by being clear about the expectations of parents versus the resources available at school. The key point is to have this all established before the student starts at school.

Safe environment

Students who show challenging behaviours benefit from feeling safe in their school, whether that be in the classroom or a room designed for students who need support. I previously described the behavioural/learning support room in the perfect world. I don't expect schools to be able to achieve this immediately, but to have a space which is safe is a good start.

In the classroom this could be an area with a tent, egg chair, bean bag, cushions etc., but remember the place should not distract other students in their learning. If it is a designated room the space should have all of the previously mentioned, but also some fun activities such as a Wii, puzzles, Lego, plasticine, computers and even a punching bag to get anger out.

One of my favourite schools to visit has what is called an enrichment room for students, but a point of difference is that it runs on a timetable. When students go to the enrichment room they are allowed five minutes of chill time, but then they must join the activity that is structured, whether it be computer learning, social skills training or problem-solving maths. Importantly, the students just cannot go out of the classroom and do nothing. What they are doing is learning in a different structure and environment.

CASE STUDY

A great example I saw of creating a safe learning environment was by a Year 10 maths teacher named David. David had a group of students who did not like school, hated maths and displayed many challenging behaviours. What David did so successfully was he set up a learning environment which was safe, but more importantly relevant to his class. A very clear list of rules and expectations was established for both teacher and students at the start and, to his credit, David listened to his students about what made things hard for them at school and in maths. From this the curriculum was established, it was communicated to the parents and the learning began.

The curriculum was structured around fun learning of life skills. The topics included:

- Planning a holiday on three different budgets with results presented on a PowerPoint. Every maths possibility had to be considered such as taxes, visas, food costs, flight costs, medical costs, insurances, etc.
- Building a house which included researching real estate, earning an income, borrowing money, design of a house and even dealing with councils.
- Fantasy football leagues for fun and banter which ran throughout the football season, teaching students how to manage money.
- Income management which included saving to buy a car, how to get a loan and money management.

Why were there no challenging behaviours in David's class? Because the learning was fun and David listened to his students.

I firmly believe that if we can set up a safe, engaging learning environment the magnitude of challenging behaviour will decrease. I ask school leaders to allow some flexibility for teachers so they can set up safe learning environments for students that take into the account the learning of all students, but also make learning fun. I want to see the fun back in teaching and learning as everyone will benefit!

Settling into routine

For some students, feeling safe in the classroom is about having a completely different routine to other students until they have settled and they are in control of their behaviour. This may also mean that a timetable is restructured to help a teacher who has the most students with challenging behaviours. In a school I visited I recommended that a class which had a significant number of students with challenging behaviours be allowed access to the gymnasium first thing in the morning every day, more time allocated in the computer hub during the afternoon and the specialist lessons to occur primarily after lunch.

Why was this? It allowed for the students to arrive at school and then go to the gym to do some hard physical activity, which enabled students to burn off excess energy. From here the class was much more settled when returning to the classroom, where structured literacy and numeracy classes took place. It was also noted that students were often tired after lunch, so time in the computer room enabled some more self-directed learning. Behaviours changed because the teacher recognised patterns and structured routines that took into account students' ability to concentrate and complete direct learning tasks

CASE STUDY

Nicholas at age seven required a completely different class routine to his peers. He was diagnosed with ADHD, but was not medicated. He had a very limited concentration span and energy to burn in the mornings. Nicholas could not sit on the carpet to listen to morning news or show and tell as he would cause chaos touching, hitting, wriggling, calling out and fiddling with anything near him.

Nicholas had a routine where when he arrived at school his job was to take all of the chairs down, turn on the class computers and feed the fish. Once this was done he could play on a computer doing a learning activity wearing headphones. When the class came in, Nicholas was engaged in an activity. The class completed the morning routine and morning talks while Nicholas was learning on the computer.

Next was fitness, which Nicholas loved and upon return Nicholas joined his peers in a structured learning lesson. During this time Nicholas received support and encouragement to stay at his desk from his teacher. It was recorded how long Nicholas could work for and reported to his parents each day. Lots of positive reinforcement was given. From here Nicholas would move between structured lessons, to working on the computer with learning tasks, based on how he was coping.

After break, learning support was provided for Nicholas and four other students in a small group setting, with the focus being on literacy. Nicholas's class also completed literacy learning at this time. Once learning support had finished, Nicholas completed a timed run outside with his time recorded. Again, burning off energy helped Nicholas to settle back into the class for the next lesson.

What was learnt was that Nicholas needed to burn off energy and have individual learning time in the classroom on a computer with headphones, but most importantly it was the routines that helped Nicholas, as he knew what was happening each day and he had fun learning without distracting others.

In some cases, changing routines is a disaster for students. Where possible I suggest that students are made to feel safe with more than one teacher. A classic example is for students with ASD, as change in routine can be very threatening for them. The idea of a relief teacher can be overwhelming, so when this happens it is important that the student can go to a safe place or classroom at the start of the day to settle in. In one school we worked to have an ASD student feeling safe with the teacher of the classroom next door. If a relief teacher was required for the class, the student would then start the day next door and slowly transition back into their classroom.

Having clear rules and boundaries

Students need to learn that there are rules and consequences at school, but this is very complicated due to the varying degrees of a diagnosed or undiagnosed condition a student has.

What I encourage teachers to do is to discuss the school and classroom rules with all of the students at the start of the year, but make them clear and in a language that students understand. Where necessary, consequences need to be put into place as the safety of all students is imperative, but sometimes the process will be slow as the student may not understand or be able to control their behaviour.

My preference is to work with rewards and lots of positive encouragement. Setting up incentives for students to change and manage their behaviour goes much further than just using negative consequences. Rewards such as extra play time, time on the computer, free play time, sport, art, choice of music in the classroom could all be considered. I find by talking to students we can get an idea of what rewards they would like and this works best.

Another strategy that can be tried is to put students into house groups or teams in which positive behaviour is rewarded. Actions such as lining up, listening, getting ready quickly, packing up quickly, can all be rewarded with points. This can lead to students helping peers in their team and the whole team working together to follow classroom rules.

Establishing rules, consequences and boundaries is what I think is the hardest part of managing challenging behaviours. Every student is different and the needs of all students need to be taken into account before any consequence is administered, but there are some rules that cannot be broken without consequence! Teacher safety and stress levels must always be considered.

Using technology for learning

As education has evolved, so has the use of technology in learning. We now have access to so much information and so many learning tools that it is understanding what is available and then learning how to use it that is important for today's teachers.

Classroom tools such as the smart board can be used for many behavioural techniques. I have seen a teacher who taught a whole lesson without speaking and just using the smart board to convey information. The students loved it as only hand signals were allowed in the classroom. It really made the students think about communication, but also gave them an understanding of what it is like to be mute.

I love to see classrooms that have at least four stand-alone computers that have relevant learning programs on them. These computers do not need to be connected to the internet as they only need to have learning programs on them with headphones attached. A task for a student in the morning can be to turn the computers on. The computers can then be used as an alternative learning method for students who have difficulty in staying with a structured lesson. Like Nicholas (as mentioned in the case study above), the idea is for students who cannot cope with the traditional classroom teaching methodologies to alternate between doing self-directed learning on the computer, having learning/ behavioural support time and joining in classroom activities.

One school community asked the parent body if it had any old computers or laptops they could have. The school offered to erase all data from the computers and then the computers would be placed in classrooms. The response from parents was overwhelming and within two weeks, every class had four stand-alone computers in it.

I see one of the aims of managing challenging behaviours is to have students spending as much time as possible in the classroom. Using technology is one way to make this happen, but like all things it must be moderate in use and not relied upon as the only behaviour management technique.

Mentoring

Students who show challenging behaviours need to have mentors who they can talk to at school. In one of my teaching roles I was also the school counsellor for students aged between 12 and 15. In many cases I was an advocate for the student and I would talk to teachers about what the student was finding difficult in the classroom and what the student would like to help them. I would then work with the teacher and student to make this happen.

As a part of prevention I teach students to have a safe place where they can go if feeling overwhelmed, angry or on the verge of a meltdown. I give them strategies to calm themselves down, but also to identify a person they feel that they can talk to about what has happened. In many cases it is the behavioural or learning support person, but I have seen schools where it is the front office staff who are brilliant at listening and calming students. The key point is that a student has someone who they trust and to whom they can go and talk, to prevent something minor turning into something drastic.

Talking to students/counselling skills

Anyone who works in a school is a potential counsellor. When working as a school counsellor I once had a grounds person come to me and explain that a student who was often in trouble and found learning difficult at school had started following him and talking to him about school and life in general. The grounds person did not know what to do.

What became clear from discussions with staff was that the student did not have many friends, was often isolated at school at break and lunchtimes, and that the student wanted to leave school. When I spoke to the student, the student explained that the grounds person was the only person at school who was nice to him and who listened without judging. What did I do?

The process was to upskill the grounds person in how to talk to the student, but to also become somewhat of a mentor. We also put in place a reward system where if the student improved classroom behaviour he could then spend the last lesson of every day working with the grounds person on general maintenance tasks. The outcome was that behaviour improved, school results improved, and the student left school and went on to complete studies in landscaping.

The point is that all school staff need some skills in talking to and listening to students. A challenge for teachers is finding the time and I will discuss this in regard to managing time shortly. What we need to do is to find ways students can convey information to us about how they are feeling so we can prevent behaviour from escalating.

I will often encourage teachers to put faces or scales up on the wall so students can use a visual to tell the teacher how they are feeling. This can allow the teacher to modify or put in place a prevention strategy. This can happen in the morning, after break or after lunch. More importantly, I ask teachers to complete the feelings process themselves, and then role model the processes they used to calm themselves or improve how they are feeling.

When I was teaching a Year 5 class of all boys, studying psychology full time and parenting two children under three, I would use the following chart every morning for my class:

- Having a great day.
- Things are good.
- Going okay.
- Be careful.
- Don't even think about it!

The boys loved it and I would explain what was happening, why I was happy, angry, tired, etc. It was the role modelling that taught the boys that it was okay to talk about how you are feeling, but more importantly what was done to improve the situation.

Not all schools have counsellors and not all students want to talk to the counsellor. This is why all schools need teachers and staff who have skills in talking to/mentoring students. Basic counselling skills for teachers /school staff is a seminar I run frequently in schools and a *Basic Counselling Book for Schools* is on its way.

Talking to and listening to students is a great way for teachers and staff to understand why a student behaves in the manner they do. If we can understand the cause we can then, where possible, put strategies into place to prevent the cause.

Learning from patterns of behaviour

A common theme from junior primary and primary school teachers is that a lot of challenging classroom behaviours occur immediately upon entering the classroom, straight after break, straight after lunch, in transition between lessons and during non-contact or specialist teacher lessons. To solve this I encourage teachers to look at particular patterns of behaviours and the causes. Then strategies can be put into place to prevent the behaviour from happening.

CASE STUDY

I worked with a seven-year-old boy who was making slow progress with his learning, and who was having enormous difficulty playing with his peers at break and lunchtimes. The end result was generally someone in tears or anger being brought into the classroom. The boy named Chris was very good at sport, with excellent hand–eye coordination and running speed.

When observing Chris in class I noticed that he took much longer than his peers to commence tasks and more often than not, he needed his teacher to explain to him on a one-to-one basis what to do and how to do it. When watching Chris at break and lunchtime I could see that he would start on the edge of play, but then join in when he knew what to do.

It appeared that Chris was a visual learner and he was having difficulty in understanding and processing verbal information. I recommended a screening test which suggested an auditory processing weakness and this was then followed with an assessment by an audiologist who diagnosed Chris as having a central auditory processing disorder.

What was happening in the yard now made complete sense. Chris could not understand the rules of the games his peers were playing. For example, the group decided the following rules:

1 Game is chasey.
2 If I catch someone we work as a pair.
3 When we catch someone the first person caught drops off and is free.
4 Not allowed to run in playground, in the passageways or behind building.

Pretty simple game, but Chris has heard the following:

1 Playing chasey.
2 Catch people.
3 Go in playground and passageway.

As you can imagine, frustration emerged and kids became angry at each other. The game would start, the kids are chasing Chris and he would go straight to the playground and climb high on the equipment. The solution was to set up very standard rules for the game and to make sure that everyone knew the rules, with extra help given to Chris in learning the rules.

When I was teaching PE, I would spend the first two lessons of the year teaching the tennis/handball game of 4 Square to each class. This was because it was a game that many children played at break or lunch and it caused arguments and stress for students and teachers alike. When everyone played by the same rules it was easy.

More often than not it was playing unstructured games at break and lunchtime that caused problems. I observed a group of Year 4 boys having a spirited game of soccer which ended badly with fighting and arguing. Why? Because the students didn't have the ability to make an umpiring decision or simply didn't like losing.

The solution was that every time there was a dispute during a game which was brought into the classroom, we would stop the game the following day ten minutes before lunch. The teacher would sit the boys down and ask them questions about the game. Questions such as what was good, what made people angry during the game etc. The boys learnt very quickly not to fight or argue and make decisions as they loved playing more than missing out on ten minutes of game time. Another solution was to provide referees who were older students and we would then organise more structured games in house teams or class teams.

A teacher once mentioned to me that his class always behaved badly when lining up (Year 6 class of 28 students). The onset of adolescent behaviour was appearing. The question I asked the teacher was, 'What is the cause and how can you make it fun?' Have a go yourself and see what you come up with. My ideas are in Appendix 7. I saw the teacher the following year and he explained how just by introducing fun into his class routines the whole atmosphere of the class changed. It all started with trying something new when lining up.

Another environmental factor that is the cause of challenging behaviours is after weekends where a student has stayed in a different house, with a parent who has vastly different rules to the house they live in during the school week – for example, parents who have separated. This is when teachers need to know the home routines so steps can be taken in advance to prepare a school routine to meet the needs of the student. Often students start school tired and unsettled due to the changes in routine they have experienced at the weekend, so a gentle start is required.

I have met a number of young students who often need to have a sleep on a Monday because they come to school so exhausted from a weekend in a house with few boundaries and rules. Further to this, at times students who are in the position where parents have separated and are fighting may need some extra help to prevent challenging behaviours from developing. Providing some school counselling support so children understand the breakdown of the relationship can be extremely helpful. It is also a good approach for the prevention of challenging behaviours.

The main point is to look for the cause of behaviours, as when we know the cause, we can prepare routines in advance to help. Learning patterns of behaviour helps teachers to plan days in advance and can be pivotal in the prevention of challenging behaviours.

Learning about the home environment

Genogram

A genogram is a very useful tool to learn about a student, which in turn can help us to understand why a student is behaving in the manner they are. To create a genogram it is best to work with a student in a one-on-one environment in a quiet and safe setting.

The genogram symbols are used to show a family structure and the genogram can be created on a whiteboard or piece of paper. The important thing is to be asking the student questions about their family structure as the links within the genogram are made. Please remember that if you detect that a student is uncomfortable in talking about their family structure you must stop.

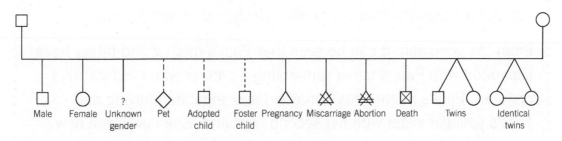

FIGURE 6.1 Symbols used to create a genogram

CASE STUDY

Paul is eight years old and new to the current school. Very little information has been included in Paul's file and his mother has not been at all forthcoming in providing a background about Paul's previous education. What is known is that Paul has attended five different schools in his three years of education and that he has an elder brother and younger sister. Paul has displayed attention-seeking behaviours, he is often tired, he is below the class level in numeracy and literacy, but at times he shows a very good understanding of learning and social awareness.

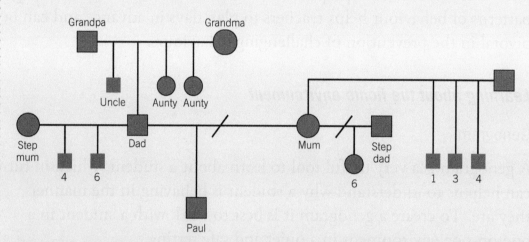

FIGURE 6.2 Genogram for Paul

A genogram is created with simple symbols representing the gender, with various lines to illustrate family relationships. Figure 6.1 illustrates basic genogram symbols with various types of individuals. Some genogram users also put circles around members who live in the same living spaces. Genograms can be prepared using a complex word processor, or a computer drawing program. There are also computer programs that are custom designed for genograms.

From the genogram it can be seen that Paul's mother and father have separated with Paul's father remarrying a partner who has two other children. Paul's mother has remarried and separated having had Paul's younger sister with her second husband. She now has a new partner who Paul and his siblings live with. Paul's mother's partner has three children from previous relationships. It is evident that Paul's grandparents are alive and that he has an uncle and two aunts.

While creating the genogram the teacher asked Paul the following questions because it is through the construction of the genogram that the information about Paul is gained. Paul was always asked to provide names and he was asked questions about his relationships with the key people in the genogram. Paul was encouraged to talk about his relationships with the people in the genogram but also what life was like living in his current arrangement.

- How many people are in your family?
- Are your mum and dad still married and living together?
- Has you mum or dad remarried?
- Are your mum and dad still with their partners?
- Has your mum a new partner?
- Do you have any brothers or sisters?
- Do you have any step brothers or sisters?
- Are your grandparents alive?
- Do you have any aunts or uncles?
- Do you live at your father's house as well as your mother's house? Is it very crowded in your mother's house? What days do you spend with your father?
- Are there different rules at your father's house compared to your mother's house?

What was learnt about Paul was that he desperately missed his father and in particular the times at weekends where he would play with his dad. Paul's father was a fly-in, fly-out worker in the mining industry, meaning that he would be home one week in four. It was also learnt that Paul did not like his mother's new partner and at his mother's house there was very little for him to do due to the house being very small and having a lot of people in it. Paul was sharing a bedroom at his mother's house but at his father's place he had his own room.

Paul also missed the contact with his grandparents (father's side) and he found it very hard to make friends at school because he feared that his mother would move again, meaning that Paul would change schools again. Paul described how hard he found parts of literacy and numeracy as he had moved schools a number of times but in the process missed large chunks of school due to not going at all. Paul did not attend kindergarten as his parents separated when he was age four and about to attend.

Paul's behaviour was attributed to the events of his childhood and the implications of his parent's separation on his education, social development and overall levels of well-being. Paul's teacher described how through talking, Paul opened up and strategies were developed to help him settle into the classroom and daily routines of school. Social skills training was provided and Paul was given lots of positive reinforcement for good behaviours. Unfortunately, Paul moved school again six months later due to his mother's relationship breaking down.

A genogram is a good way of getting to know a student and then using the information to work out why they may behave as they do. It also allows for a good relationship to develop between the teacher and student due to the opportunity for a one-to-one chat.

Individual patterns on environment or medication

As previously mentioned, learning about a student's environment can go a long way towards planning for and preventing behaviours. What is also helpful is for teachers to know if students are on any prescribed medication, but also how the medication can impact upon behaviour at school. The most common form of medication I have observed is for ADHD.

If a teacher is concerned that a student is showing signs of ADHD and challenging behaviours are presenting, the first step is to raise concerns with the parents. From there checklists can be completed. What I would suggest then, if parents are supportive, is a diet trial to see if changing a child's diet impacts upon behaviour. I also suggest looking at exercise and sleep patterns as a part of this process.

Once this has been trialled and the symptoms are all still present I recommend paediatric involvement. If medication is then prescribed it is important that the teacher understands not only what the medication is, but also how it impacts upon the behaviour of the student. This is a good time to keep some records on levels of concentration, work output and overall behaviours. These records can be given to parents to present to the paediatrician for the first review.

With some medication the effect can wear off and this is important for teachers to understand because as the medication wears off, challenging behaviours can reappear. This means planning for the change in behaviours. What also helps is to plan to have the more high-intensity literacy and numeracy lessons while the medication is in effect and lessons such as computer studies, physical education and art when the medication has no effect. The best thing is for the teacher to understand the learning needs of the student and plan accordingly. The aim would be to plan the lessons the student likes and can focus on when the medication is not in effect.

Helping students at break and lunch

A great cause of so much stress for teachers and students alike are the behaviours that occur and the flow of consequences as a result of break and lunchtime play. I have previously mentioned Chris as an example of a student who had so much difficulty in playing with peers. I have also noticed that many students with ASD also find break and lunchtime very challenging, which then leads to high levels of teacher time being needed to help and assist the student.

I would not have endorsed the following solution 12 months ago, but I have changed my position due to not only learning more, but also by having a go to see what happened when I suggested a trial of a Minecraft club. What the staff and I did in a school was to set up a Minecraft club every Monday, Wednesday and Friday in a computer lab at school, with restricted student access on Monday and Wednesday.

What we discovered was that students who were lost at break and lunchtime now had a place to go where they could do something they liked and in many cases were very good at. Part of the club also revolved around talking about Minecraft and in students working together to help each other.

The end result was that students of different ages made friends who they could meet at break and lunchtime to talk about a common interest. An interesting note to this story was that the teacher then opened up the room on Tuesday and Thursdays, but the focus of these days was the learning of robotics. The same students all attended, but now the focus was shifting. In talking to the teacher I was made aware that the plan was eventually to only have two days of Minecraft and more time on robotics and the development of a remote-controlled boat to compete in a university challenge.

The challenging behaviours associated with not knowing how to play or having anyone to play with was removed by giving the students something to do at lunchtimes. A big challenge for teachers and staff alike is the management of break and lunchtime yard behaviours. Some tips that can help:

- Teach students a standard set of rules for games as then students know and understand how to play.
- Teach problem-solving skills to students. If a dispute occurs in the game or play, how is it solved?
- Have consequences for consistent disputed play, such as finishing the game early to evaluate the play.
- Have older students act as mentors in games for younger students. School or house leaders can fill this role as a part of their leadership development, but must be trained first.
- Organise for structured games at lunchtime. House games, class games, staff versus student games can all be played at break and lunchtimes and students love this. I know this can mean more work for teachers, but the plus side is less behavioural disputes at break and lunchtimes.

I think teaching students to be able to win and lose is important, as I see some students display challenging behaviour when they lose, such as tantrums or physical anger towards another student. From teachers' perspective, the lesson of learning how to win and lose is important and needs to be encouraged.

Many challenging behaviours can be prevented by giving students a place to belong to, activities to do at break and lunchtime and by educating students on how to play with each other in a competitive game with the fun being in playing, while trying to win. This is not easy, but a worthy challenge.

Teaching social skills

The teaching of social skills is something I am seeing needs to be done more and more in schools. Today's children are spending so much more time using technology than yesterday's students and in doing so they are losing the skills of how to interact and play with each other. The end result of this is that students fight and argue, particularly when things do not go their way.

Social skills can be taught through role modelling, structured lessons, and also during free play for students. Playing board games, card games and sporting games can all help in the teaching of social skills. Too often students do not have the skills and conflict results. Students with ASD find learning social skills particularly difficult and a large amount of work needs to be put into the teaching of social skills at a young age.

A consideration for schools is to have specific times when students who have difficulty with social skills are withdrawn from class and then receive specific social skills training relevant to their age and needs. Students can also be supported at break and lunchtime by having an older buddy, school leaders watching out for students, or being provided with a safe place to go at these times.

The schools that I see that cater the best for the teaching of social skills are ones that have a safe place for students to go at break and lunchtimes where they can play with and talk to fellow students, for example, the Minecraft club. There are many social skills programmes available and all can be considered, but please be aware of costs to parents before suggesting these alternatives.

Teaching life skills

A great challenge in middle and high school is differentiating the curriculum. When we have 13-, 14- and 15-year-old students who are not engaged in learning purely because they cannot access the curriculum, we generally see a decline in classroom behaviour, which is the fight or flight process at work. Yet so many students are forced to do subjects in which they have neither interest nor cognitive ability to succeed.

I would love to see students given more choices in their curriculum at an earlier age. At age 14 a student in conjunction with parents and teachers should be able to make a decision to proceed into an educational pathway where they are taught life skills with the aim being to prepare the student to transition from school into the workforce. Schools could be designed purely for this purpose with students having a choice of what educational pathway they would like. The choice would be guided by discussions between parents, teachers and the student. In doing this we would see happier students and less challenging behaviours in the classroom.

Students who have a pathway and purpose at school show less challenging behaviours because they feel a value in education. More choices for students, more specifically created schools and pathways available upon leaving school are what we need.

Promoting health in students

I have talked about the importance of communication to parents and as a part of this I see helping parents to make healthy changes with their children as helpful in managing behaviours. This, of course, can be a delicate process, as some parents do not want to be told how to parent. So how do we get parents involved in school communities to help their children?

Some activities to try are:

- Regular meetings with parents and staff in both a formal and informal setting. This can be at community days, school breakfasts, picnics etc.
- Inviting parents onto school groups as volunteers. It is often the volunteers that make excellent mentors for students with challenging behaviours.
- Have professionals visit the school to talk to parents.

- Provide information to parents through email, newsletter or the school website about themes running in the school. It might be good manners week, or healthy eating week, but advising parents is good so they can try to help at home.
- Refer parents to specialist support. Schools need to have a list of professionals to which they can guide parents.
- Talk to parents about working on changing one behaviour at a time. For many parents it is just too hard, so they let the behaviours continue and then the flow-on effect is brought to school.

Schools need parents on board when managing challenging behaviours and to achieve this, staff and teachers need to be welcoming and not threatening, as many parents are struggling enough at home to manage the child. The last thing the parent needs is more criticism from teachers and staff. Positive support is the best method. Get the parents onside and work together to change behaviours, one at a time.

Classroom strategies for teachers

The following ideas are for teachers to work towards implementing within their classrooms. Some of the ideas require working with fellow staff members and a supportive school community; however, the ideas are more classroom based.

Setting up times to talk

A big part of managing challenging behaviour for teachers is finding the time to be able to talk to the students to address the reoccurring behaviour. In most classrooms and with the loaded-up curriculum it is very difficult to find the time. To counter this I encourage teachers to establish high-intensity versus low-intensity teaching times.

This means that when we know that there is a likelihood of challenging behaviour occurring due to known the patterns, it is good to have a low-intensity teaching lesson where students are completing primarily self-directed learning tasks. This gives teachers time to talk to students and address the behaviour.

Typical low-intensity teaching subjects are silent reading, group activities such as board games or problem solving, computing, art or watching an educational programme on the smart board or TV. This does not mean that teachers don't teach the class, but what it means is students are engaged in a quiet learning task so the teacher can spend time and talk to a student. Typical low-intensity teaching times are after lunch, after break or after a non-contact teaching lesson.

I also think that this is integral to teacher well-being. Teachers need to have low-intensity teaching times because if you only go at high intensity you will burn out.

Preparing for battles

This is an interesting concept. Sometimes we have to have battles with students because they have not done what is required of them, whether that be in regard to completing school work or general behaviour. The mistake most teachers make is that they pick the wrong battles and have them at the wrong times.

With many students with challenging behaviours some battles are simply not worth having. Always ask, 'Is the behaviour of the student impacting upon the learning of others?' If not, don't pick the battle, but store it away until the right time and when you are ready for the battle.

To get ready for a battle I encourage teachers and staff to prepare. This means alerting as many possible staff as needed to the fact that you are going to challenge a student and the result could be chaotic, so best all be ready. The advantage here is that the student does not know it is coming, but the staff do.

Also when having battles there is no point in having it at 9.05 am when there is so much time ahead. Diffuse the behaviour, but at 2.40 pm when the class is about to do a fun activity, then have the battle. If the activity is one the student loves and good rapport has been established, chances are the battle won't amount to much. What does need to happen is that people are ready and aware just in case.

The key point is to not pick pointless battles with students that will lead to disputes that disrupt the learning of the class. The best thing to do is to wait for the right moment and then challenge the student.

Building self-esteem

I wish I could create a self-esteem injection for students. The sad thing is that some schools seem to simply beat self-esteem out of students without giving much thought as to how to build self-esteem up. I understand that we need to have structure, academic assessment and push students to achieve to the best of their ability, but I think this gets blurred far too often. Students who are finding learning difficult, have a diagnosed condition or bring emotional baggage with them to school are already at risk of having low self-esteem. The challenge is to build them up.

The following are simple ways to build up the self-esteem of students, which leads to better rapport with teachers and less challenging behaviours:

- Know your students, what they like, are good at, sporting team they follow, TV show they like etc. At the start of the year it is a great idea for teachers to do a 'get to know your students' questionnaire as this gives teachers an insight as to what a student likes. The teacher can then talk about the results, building rapport.
- Think carefully about the language used when talking to students. Is the language negative, critical or positive? Praise builds self-esteem, but also makes students feel good about being in the classroom.
- Find things a student is good at and acknowledge it where possible. Congratulate students on art work, music, sport, academic achievement etc., sometimes in public and sometimes one to one. Students feel good when they are recognised as being good at something.
- Allow students the opportunity to show their strengths within the curriculum where possible. This can mean some creative timetabling, but it is worth it in managing behaviours.

The point is that students who have a healthy self-esteem are less likely to have challenging behaviours at school because they feel good about being there.

Teacher methodology – being organised

So much of managing challenging behaviour at school falls back onto the teachers, and because of this, it is important that teachers are on the ball, organised and prepared for their classes.

CASE STUDY

I recently visited a Year 9 class where I sat in as an observer. Fifteen students (11 boys, 4 girls) were doing a home economics lesson in sewing. The lesson was fine until it got to the point that the students needed to use the sewing machines. The problem was that there were only five sewing machines in the room. This meant that potentially there would be ten students waiting around with nothing to do. The result is predictable. The boys became restless with freedom to move around and talk. While the teacher was helping students with the use of machines, chaos broke out.

What was needed was better planning. Year 9 boys need to be kept busy. A further mistake by the teacher was that she had her back to the class when helping students on the machines due to the position of the machines. Thus we can see, planning in the set-up of the room is as important as the planning of the lesson.

Some simple teaching methodologies need to be adhered to, such as never turn your back on students and keep Year 9 boys busy! As a part of organisation, teachers can ensure computers are turned on, the lesson timetable is on the board, a safe place is set up and stations for group work are set up. Time consuming yes, but this is where students can help with the set-up as a part of building teacher/student rapport and student self-esteem.

Teachers should be evaluated, but it needs to be done constructively and with the aim of improving the quality of teaching. I like the idea of experienced teachers spending time in classrooms, evaluating and giving feedback. One concern that has arisen from numerous teacher meetings about students is why it is that a number of students only show challenging behaviours in one or two classes, but in all of the other classes they are fine. What is the difference between teachers? This is where teachers can help each other and consistent methodologies can be put into place in schools.

Rapport

Building rapport with students is what I believe to be the most important way to manage any classroom or school behaviour. When I am talking to parents, far too often I hear that a student does not want to go to school. All enthusiasm for learning is lost and as a result the disruptive or work avoidance behaviours appear.

What I love to see is students who arrive every day for school with a smile (sometimes hard for teenagers), but more importantly who are greeted by the school staff using their name. I love to walk into schools and see principals standing at the gate saying good morning to students, having a quip about a football result, congratulating a student on a piece of art or a recent musical performance or even making a positive comment to a student about their behaviour on the previous day. Students then feel valued and enthusiasm for learning grows.

We must work at building rapport in schools. This is much easier in smaller schools but so much harder in high schools due to the large volume of students with which many teachers work. However, there are ways to develop rapport and the following are some ideas to try:

Learning students' names

Learning students' names is paramount to building rapport but also in managing behaviours. For a teacher this takes time but the investment is well worth it. An idea to try: ask students to complete an interest questionnaire providing information about themselves (see Appendix 5 for an example and feel free to use it).

For high school students learning names takes longer. An idea to try in the first week is to sit the students in alphabetical order and have a chart on your desk so you can quickly learn and use the names of students. Playing name games or looking at school photographs in advance can also help teachers to remember names.

Learning about students' interests

I once learnt that a student who would challenge teachers with his behaviour loved *The Simpsons*. In order to build rapport I watched a couple of episodes so I could then talk to the student about the show. Every morning from then on, the student would give me a quick rundown on the previous night's episode. I would ask the student to rate it out of ten (introducing scaling techniques to the student) and ask why it was scored as it was. We were now talking and when challenging behaviours presented we could talk with ease. The result was a decrease in challenging behaviours. It also helped that I had some Simpsons juggling balls in my office which the student loved. I taught the student to juggle, which led to more rapport being established.

It can take time to learn about a student's interests but it is well worth the investment. Appendix 6 is a sentence completion test. This is a good way of learning about a student by asking them to complete the questionnaire, writing down the first thing that comes into their head in response to the words at the start of the sentence. It is designed to be done quickly by students and it is a great way to learn about what a student is thinking.

Role modelling good behaviours

As teachers I think it is important to role model good behaviours. Part of this is also talking about or demonstrating your interests to the students. This can be done by having some pictures or items that you like in your classroom so students can see what you are interested in. When the opportunity presents, show the students your interests. Days such as Wear Your Team Colours are a great opportunity to show what team you support and to create some healthy banter with students, parents and fellow staff. Play in staff versus students sports games, join the school choir or band, and support school events as these all let students see that, as teachers, we have interests as well.

Talk to students in the yard

Any yard duty provides the perfect opportunity to have a quick chat to a student. It is often in the yard where you can congratulate the student on an achievement, provide feedback about behaviour, join in a game or just take the time to talk to students about interests. When students know your interests they are more likely to approach you in the yard for a chat. I will not forget the ribbing I used to receive every Monday morning when I walked through the yard and my team had lost, but also the jeers when I would wear my team's jumper to school. The students loved it as much as I did.

Perception of the teacher as a person

Part of building rapport is the perception that teachers create about themselves for students. I always ask teachers to answer this question honestly: 'How do students perceive me? Am I perceived as friendly, positive, enthusiastic, committed or conversely as negative, grumpy, boring and unapproachable?' I encourage teachers to consider this question and then set three strategies to improve the perception students have of them. Part of this is often the idea of becoming a positive person. This starts with how we, as teachers, respond to students. Positive responses such as 'Good effort', 'I like your thinking', 'Good thought', 'Great idea' etc. create such a positive environment. Criticism needs to be given but this should be done through the 'criticism sandwich' which is positive comment, negative or improvement comment and then positive comment. I encourage teachers to become positive role models through actions and words.

Show enthusiasm

I encourage all teachers to get involved. Having two children who have now finished school I often asked them what they appreciated most about their teachers. A consistent answer has been not only the enthusiasm shown by their teachers about the subjects that they taught to the students, but also to everything related to the school. Having teachers who enthusiastically greet students, take on every new topic to be taught with genuine gusto and who clearly love their jobs goes a long way in developing rapport and an enthusiasm for learning.

Laugh, crack jokes

Darren Lehmann, coach of the Australian cricket team, has introduced the rule that every training session and meeting starts with a joke. A player is given the task of telling the joke. He does this to break the ice, lighten the mood of the group and also on most occasions it allows everyone to have a laugh. All humans benefit from laughing. So my suggestion is to start a lesson or end the day with 'joke of the day'. Students can be asked to tell the joke as this develops public speaking. With the use of technology jokes are easy to find, and it is a good way to make students laugh.

In one school a teacher assigned a student with ASD the task of finding a funny YouTube clip for the staff to watch every Monday to start the week and every Friday to end the week. This automatically established rapport for the teacher but it also gave the ASD student a very healthy dose of self-esteem. The student was asked lots of questions by peers about the clips but also the ASD student got to talk to peers about his interest, which was computers. Other students were also given the opportunity to share clips, but most importantly everyone laughed. The students perceived the teachers as fun and the teachers had great rapport with the students due to the laughter.

Show humility and honesty

As teachers we need to show humility. This is a part of role modelling for students. To be honest enough to admit to mistakes and to talk to students about how we are feeling shows that we are human and also makes us much more approachable to students. Our students can see that we experience many of the same emotions that they do. In the process we can teach students coping strategies. Humility and honesty are two qualities that build rapport.

Demonstrate listening and problem-solving behaviours

This goes a long way to building rapport with students as when we show listening behaviours, students learn that we value them and want to work with them. Too often in a busy teaching environment teachers simply do not take the time to listen to students. Making time during the day to listen to students should be a priority for building rapport. It is important to concurrently demonstrate both listening behaviours and problem-solving behaviours. Sitting down and listening to a student and then working with them to solve problems builds rapport. A very simple problem-solving model is as follows:

- Listen to the student describe what the problem is. Ask lots of questions but listen without telling the student what to do.
- Ask the student to score the problem out of ten for severity. If the student says eight out of ten, ask what could be done to reduce the score to six out of ten. Alternatively, ask the student, 'If I waved my magic wand and did my magic, what would change?' We are asking the student to describe the changes.
- Ask, 'What can we do to make these changes happen?'
- Ask, 'Who can help you make the changes happen?'
- If the student is unsure of how to make the changes happen we can make suggestions.
- Create a plan to make the changes happen.
- Follow up with the student and use lots of positive reinforcement to encourage the student to keep working on changing the behaviour. Sometimes there will not be success and this is when lots of encouragement is needed to motivate the student to keep trying.

Using this listening and problem-solving model shows students that we are really trying to help them and this creates good rapport which then reduces problematic behaviour.

Smile

This goes without saying. It is very important in building rapport with students. I always ask teachers to have three rapport-building behaviours they are focusing on each week and smiling is a very simple one to include. The body language of teachers can do so much to build rapport. The nod in the yard, a simple thumbs up or smile shows we care and are interested in a student.

Set themes

As mentioned, students don't remember a lot about their education, but they remember the significant events. Having themes in a classroom allows the creation of memories for students but also builds rapport. Themes that incorporate students' interests are even better as the students can work with the teacher to create the theme and classroom events for the week.

An example might be when the Olympic Games are on, so the classroom theme is the Olympics. Subjects get transformed into events with medals being awarded, team competitions and each group of students adopting a country. The curriculum revolves around the Olympics. This can be done with a variety of events such as elections, remembrance days, holidays and, of course, major sporting events. For teachers it is about being creative while involving students in the planning.

Extra-curricular activities

So many strong teacher–student relationships are built through the extra-curricular activities the teacher gets involved in at school. I once worked with a student who displayed challenging behaviours in every subject except for history, which was quite odd as the student had a specific learning disability and history was a struggle. Why was the student well-behaved in history? The reason was that the teacher coached the school football team and the student was a player in the team. The student respected the teacher because the teacher was his coach.

Much is gained for teachers when it comes to building rapport with students by doing extra-curricular activities such as school camps, drama productions, sport, music, clubs of any kind etc. Students remember the extra things teachers do and the respect and rapport that is established generally lasts a lifetime.

Class environment

The classroom environment helps to build rapport and this goes with establishing themes. A classroom that is welcoming, engaging and busy grants the teacher means in which to talk to students. An environment that allows students to bring items of interest, wear interesting clothes at specified times and has a flexible learning environment builds rapport between students and the teacher and in turn reduces problematic behaviours. Encouraging the students to get involved in the creation of the rules and environment also helps with rapport and behaviour.

Parents

A classroom and school will always function much better when parents are involved and supportive. Thus building rapport with parents is important. It is hard enough to learn the names of students as well as parents but I encourage teachers to try. Use name tags or labels to help at community events. This not only helps us as teachers but it also helps parents to learn and remember the names of fellow class parents. Encourage parents to visit the classroom whenever possible and be clear about expectations. A positive relationship with parents is critical when managing challenging behaviours.

Building rapport with students can be done in many ways yet in the busyness of a school day, week and term it is often overlooked. If rapport can be established at the start of the year, classroom management will become much easier for all teachers. Know your students and let them get to know you.

Engaging curriculum

Having an engaging curriculum that is accessible to students is important in managing student behaviour. When students can engage in the curriculum they are less likely to be disruptive. Creating an engaging curriculum is a challenge as often classrooms have many constraints which limit the ability to change the curriculum to meet the needs of the students.

In order to create an engaging curriculum, schools need to make decisions with regard to their policies on how classrooms will be structured. Will students be grouped by ability level, gender or interest, or be in a classroom with their class group not factoring in any of the previous grouping ideas? If students are not grouped it does become challenging as teachers then have to adjust and modify the curriculum so all students can achieve the learning outcome. This is a lot of work for teachers. Regardless of this, here are some ideas to make the curriculum interesting and one that creates enthusiasm for learning:

Interesting

Choose interesting topics for the students that are relevant to their age and interest.

Learn in different ways

Use various methods for learning such as reading, listening, researching on the internet, interviewing people, creating presentations or movies, giving oral presentations, building models etc. The important requirement is that students can demonstrate their learning. We must remember that students learn in many different ways and giving alternatives helps some students (particularly those who have a specific learning disability or an ASD student) to show they have learnt about a topic. There will always be time for tests, assignments and exams, but mixing it up increases engagement.

Environment

The environment allows students to work both inside and outside of the classroom. Here are some ideas:

- Maths outside on a wall with bricks?
- Poetry written on school walls in chalk for everyone to read.
- Silent reading outside under a tree.
- Trips to the museum for history.
- Field trips for geography.
- Guest speakers on a topic.
- Science experiments out in the middle of the playground (rocket work).
- Changing the environment can change the attitude of students and make the curriculum far more attractive to students

Group work

Work in groups when appropriate. This allows students to work with friends or even people they do not know well. It can also allow students who find the work easier to help students who find it harder. Group work can be very helpful for ASD students or even defiant students. Teaching cooperation through group work is a beneficial skill for students to learn but group work is also very valuable in helping some students access the curriculum.

Fun

Make the curriculum enjoyable. Again, this can be challenging due to educational constraints; however, it is by using a variety of learning tools that we can make learning fun. Think about the environment, the delivery of materials, and the end result and always look at ways of making it fun. Do some research on a topic or ask students to do the research. Use tools such as Google to look for funny and different ways to present information.

Classroom teachers and school staff do not have to be comedians, but a good sense of humour does help. Look for jokes, plays on words, tell funny stories, and use drama to illustrate a point but where possible make it fun. Students will become much more engaged in lessons and the curriculum when it is fun. Start and finish the day with a joke. Read funny books to your class, wear interesting clothing, but make the day enjoyable.

Finally, I think that all teachers should attend professional development on a regular basis to learn new methods for delivering the curriculum to students. Far too many teachers have been teaching the same thing the same way for far too long and it is boring. Attending professional development or having staff professional development days where teachers can discuss the delivery of the curriculum will certainly help a school to prepare and deliver a fun, engaging curriculum.

The start of the year – the two tough weeks

The start of the year is the opportunity to set the expectations of how a classroom is going to function. It is amazing how quickly students of all ages pick up that the teacher is serious about the rules of a class and the consequences. It is also the opportunity for teachers to show that they are not going to be the students' friend, but their teacher. I have seen some young teachers in middle and high schools who want to be seen as cool by the students and the students end up walking all over them. The first two weeks set the standards. The following is an example of how teachers, particularly high school teachers, can set up for the start of the year.

- Get background information on the behavioural and learning needs of students.
- Arrange desks as required. Use single file so students cannot interact too much at the start.
- Appoint names to desks so students are told where to sit. Chart map on board for students to see. This allows learning of names much easier. Alphabetical order really helps.

- Establish classroom rules.
- Have lots of work ready to go at the start.
- Be ready to keep students in at break and lunchtime to complete work.
- Be ready to communicate to parents any behavioural concerns.

When the students realise that you are serious about the rules and expectations they will adapt very quickly. Like so many students, if you give an inch, they will take a mile and then the management of the class and rules becomes blurred. This then leads to challenging behaviours increasing. Set the standard at the start. As one of my former colleagues used to say, 'Don't smile until you've had 10 weeks with your class'.

Once the students have settled, then the organisation of the classroom can change. Students can sit in groups, with friends and talk, but the expectations of behaviour remain the same. I do encourage teachers to constantly rearrange the room and seating of students depending on the lesson.

As you will now understand, there are many ways to manage a student's behaviour at school and in the classroom. What I trust is also clear is how important the building of relationships is with students. At the core of managing challenging behaviours is being able to build good working relationships with students. In most cases it is this strong relationship that will go a very long way in helping a student to modify their behaviour at school and in the classroom because the student respects you.

I find building relationships and working with children in managing challenging behaviours is very rewarding but also extremely difficult at times. However, if you think working with children is hard, step back and reflect how much harder it is to work with many of the parents who have children with challenging behaviours. In so many cases it is the parents who we first need to work with. Chapter 7 provides some insights as to how we can develop good relationships with parents but also engage them in the process of modifying challenging behaviours.

7 Working with parents

Communication with parents to help in behaviour management

Talking to parents about their child's behaviour can be very challenging; however, it is necessary to help facilitate behavioural change. There are a number of considerations teachers and schools need to make before communicating with parents. This then needs to be taken further when cooperative plans are put into place between parents and students to manage and change students' behaviours.

Before communicating with parents

When considering alerting parents to concerning behaviours it is important for teachers and school staff to consider the following points:

- Have parents previously been informed of the concerns?
- What information has been presented to parents in the past?
- How have parents reacted to any information regarding behaviour?
- What is known about the parents' ability to comprehend and act on the information that will be presented to them?

I raise these concerns as I have met teachers who have described how devastated parents have been when presented with behaviour concerns because of having siblings who have shown the same behavioural patterns. I have heard teachers report how parents have dismissed concerns with phrases such as 'not a concern at home' or 'he is just a typical boy'. There have also been some parents who simply do not care and see it as the school's problem, so the school can deal with it. Knowing the parents and having a good rapport with them is very important when communicating any behavioural concerns.

The method of communication

Having established that a conversation is needed with parents regarding behaviour, it is important to consider how the communication will take place. Ideally, we would be able to sit down with parents in an interview setting and talk through the behaviours that present. I encourage teachers and school staff to try to put themselves in the position of the parents when considering the communication means. This is primarily due to some parents only ever receiving what they perceive to be bad news from schools and thus being defensive when they are contacted.

A phone conversation, quick chat at drop-off or pick-up, or an email asking parents to make a time to sit down and chat is the first step. At any meeting, positive behaviours must also be raised and the language used when talking to parents should be non-threatening, saying, 'We are concerned about John in the classroom as at times he is doing …, have you noticed this at home?' I see this as a much better way to start the conversation, rather than automatically handing parents a checklist or by suggesting a student is on the autistic spectrum. The way we communicate to parents can be the difference between parents working with us or against us. Staff training in communication with parents is also advised.

It is also very important to follow up with parents once communication has begun. This can easily be done through email or phone contact. Always be cautious about sending information home with students as it may not reach the destination or the student may read it.

Working together and supporting parents when changing behaviour

When we have parents on board and supporting behavioural change we must always remember the capacity of the parents to help with the change. Often the environment a student lives in makes behavioural change very difficult. I would always recommend that the focus be on changing one behaviour at a time. As a part of this process schools can provide parents with help and tips that they can implement at home.

An example scenario could be a student is tired at school and as a result concentration and behaviour drops off as the day progresses. The aim is to help parents facilitate better sleeping patterns and some advice for parents could be as follows:

- Increase the amount of exercise done after school.
- Have a no sugar intake after 6 pm.
- Turn off all TV/computer/gaming at 8 pm.
- No video/screens/gaming allowed in bedroom.
- Encourage reading before bed.
- Set up a very standard bed routine.
- Start the bed routine at same time every night.
- Go to bed at the same time every night.

There are a lot of things that can be tried, but what schools can do is support parents by helping parents to work on one thing at a time. For example, the teacher could ensure that a student does not need the internet to complete homework, while parents are working on turning off all screens/video games. The class might be doing a healthy eating experiment that all students are involved in to reduce sugar. There might be a reading challenge for a week. The key thing is that schools and parents can work together to change behaviours.

I have visited schools that now have homework clubs as a means of helping parents control internet/gaming addictions. Schools and teachers are not the parents, but behaviour management and change can be a combined process and I certainly believe that when both parties are on the same page the chance of success increases significantly.

Information to help parents with behaviours/setting up for success

I like the idea of schools providing information to parents on how they can help to set their child up for success at school. This can be done through newsletters, parent–teacher meetings or through having guest speakers visiting the schools. With having guest speakers the unfortunate outcome is that it is generally the parents who are doing the right things who attend and the parents who need the most support are absent. However, we need to persevere.

The following points are, I believe, the key ones in helping parents set their children up for success. As a school we can make these recommendations for parents:

- Sleep.
- Diet.
- Routine for homework, bedtimes, relaxation times etc.
- Control of technology by parents.
- Role-modelling behaviours and emotions from parents to children.
- How to listen to children.
- How to talk to our children.
- How to implement consequences, both positive and negative.

Providing a list of recommended professional external support is also useful for parents.

All of the recommendations for parents can be reviewed at different points through the various forms of communication that schools have with parents. The key is for schools to always keep trying and to keep the lines of communication open between parents and teachers.

Working with parents is critical to modifying challenging behaviours in schools, as when we have parents working with us we are able to have strategies implemented at home and at school. The challenge in a school is engaging the parents to work with us, but at times in also understanding that our processes are in the best interest of their child. Good communication skills and patience are important. My last recommendation is to have a glass of empathy every morning with breakfast as we need to be able to put ourselves in the position of the parent who is battling as much as we are to manage the behaviour of their child. The stress associated with this can be enormous for parents and some empathy from schools and teachers makes a great difference.

A school that manages challenging behaviours well has good resources, an environment with spaces to support students, a well-structured timetable, parents who are supportive of the processes implemented by the school, and staff who are committed to supporting and working with all students who have challenging behaviours. Unfortunately, this can be a challenge in schools. In Chapter 8 I will describe ways in which schools can get all staff on the same page and working successfully with students who have challenging behaviours.

8 | Getting staff on board

Getting all staff members to support behaviour change can often be a challenge as there are still teachers who are very much old school; rather than try to understand the student, they will simply dismiss the student as wilful and treat them as naughty. The most effective behaviour change is made when all staff are working together to help students. How can we do this?

- Staff professional development is critical as this allows teachers to understand behaviours, but also develop strategies to manage.
- Giving staff support in the classroom when needed.
- Setting up the classroom to support students to make teaching easier for teachers.
- Providing teachers with the time to talk to each other about developing strategies.
- Making staff members feel valued by the school and community. I visited a school where the parent body bought an extremely good coffee machine for the staff – a gesture that has created a great relationship.

Many of the above have been previously mentioned, but they are very important. Good schools have staff on board all working together. While considering this we must never forget that teachers are our most vital resource and we need to look after them. Teacher well-being is a big part in managing challenging behaviours as in any profession. When tired and stressed we do not function anywhere near as well as we need to and, as a result, it gets increasingly harder to keep on top of the day-to-day challenges that present.

There are many strategies to try, and this is the key – try to see what happens. It is impossible to implement all of the changes suggested in a single year, but what I encourage is to move forward step by step. The staff can select some of the ideas that they believe can be put into place at school and then create a plan to make it happen. This is an excellent project for a staff development day. This way the staff has ownership, making it more likely to be effective. The staff body is a school's biggest asset, and as such we must work to look after our staff. Caring for the carer, or teacher well-being, must be made a priority in all schools and, in particular, schools and classes that have challenging behaviours in them.

Teacher well-being/caring for the carer

I meet many teachers through my work in schools and one particular behaviour pattern which I see as common to teachers is that so many of them don't sleep well during the school term. It seems that a large majority of teachers go to bed late, wake up around 2.30 am thinking about school or students for a couple of hours, fall back to sleep around 4.30 and then the alarm goes off at 6.30. A lot of teachers are very tired and an increase in expectation and workload is not helping. So what do we need to do?

The first thing teachers need is to be able to identify the signs of stress/ work burnout. The following are typical signs of teacher stress:

- Not wanting to go to school in the morning.
- Having disrupted sleep during school terms.
- Having headaches or body pains only when at school.
- Withdrawing from interactions with school peers.
- Avoiding the school staffroom.
- Having emotional fluctuations while at school.
- Talking about school too much to your partner and friends.
- Feeling guilty about going home early when school work is not marked.
- Putting school work before caring for yourself or attending social outings with friends or family.

Being able to identify the triggers for stress is also important for teachers so strategies can be put in place to reduce the causes. The following are typical causes associated with teacher stress:

- Being under constant pressure to produce results within a set time.
- Work requiring lots of energy over a long time.
- Performing tasks which are repeated over and over again.

- A lack of trust between individuals and others.
- Working under difficult circumstances with difficult groups.
- Having unresolved personal conflicts with parents, students or staff.
- Having unrealistic performance targets set.
- Inadequate training for tasks.
- Insufficient resources.
- Insufficient time.
- No support or encouragement from colleagues or management.
- Being subjected to criticism, humiliation or bullying at work.
- Personal needs not being met.
- Giving large amounts of personal and emotional energy to others without results.

How many signs and causes can you identify that impact upon you?

Once we have identified that we are experiencing stress, the next stage is to put strategies into place that help us to reduce stress, become proactive in helping us to care for ourselves, and prevent stress. A key factor in this is support from the principal and colleagues. The following are very good ways teachers can reduce personal stress levels, while also supporting colleagues.

What can schools do to improve well-being of staff?

Schools can try to implement some or, in a perfect world, all of the following:

Internal staff welfare service

Employers can provide an internal staff welfare service staffed by experienced personnel with specialist skills who have developed expertise in the areas of staff welfare and well-being. Staff welfare officers provide an easily accessible, confidential welfare support service for teachers who are experiencing problems arising from work, personal, domestic or social situations.

Staff welfare officers are available to meet confidentially one to one with individual teachers to offer welfare guidance and support. They can draw on an extensive knowledge of the education sector and teaching terms and conditions of service and are well-placed to source a broad range of education support services to assist in the resolution of work-related stress issues. Staff welfare officers can facilitate discussion as appropriate between relevant individuals (e.g. teachers, principals, trade union representatives, human resource staff) to help address teachers' welfare concerns at work.

Staff welfare officers have developed knowledge of and contacts with a broad range of support organisations and, where appropriate, can assist the individual teacher to identify and access external specialist organisations to seek the right kind of professional help to solve the problem.

The staff welfare service also has a role to promote teacher health and well-being at work through awareness-raising and training.

External counselling service and telephone care-line

In addition to the staff welfare service, the employer can provide access to an external counselling service for teaching staff. This is provided by a regional network of professionally qualified counsellors who are external to the employer.

The service consists of a 24-hour free telephone care-line manned by qualified counsellors and normally up to four face-to-face counselling sessions (or more in exceptional circumstances) are available. It is confidential and independent and is funded by the employing authorities.

It is the responsibility of the employer and school principals to raise teacher awareness of both these welfare support services.

Flexible working arrangements

A comprehensive set of flexible working arrangements can be negotiated for teachers:

- Days off to attend appointments or special events.
- Job Share Scheme.
- Career Break Scheme.
- Flexible Working Scheme.
- Temporary Variation of Contract.

Managing workload

It is widely accepted that efforts need to be made to reduce bureaucratic burden and allow teachers the time to focus on their core business of teaching and learning.

Promoting good health

Excellent work has been done in promoting health and well-being for pupils in some schools. Employers have in some cases been involved in organising health promotion events for schools or clusters of schools.

Good health promotion emphasises the need for early detection of health problems. Teachers should be encouraged to take responsibility for their own health and should seek medical advice at an early stage when they have health concerns. Teachers' attendance for health checks could be facilitated by their employer.

Encouraging health professionals to visit the school to provide services to staff can also help in the promotion of good health. Having a massage therapist visit the school on certain days so teachers can book in a massage in their free time or a yoga teacher visiting to commence a class after school are just a couple of possible options for schools to consider.

Encouraging teachers to participate in community fitness events or entering a staff team into a community sports competition are also excellent ways for staff to build good healthy routines. It also gives the staff something to talk about to their students – perfect role modelling!

Winding down and retirement

There is a possibility of developing a 'winding-down' scheme for teachers in their last few years of service, for those who may find it difficult to sustain a full teaching commitment. A winding-down scheme would allow teachers to reduce their hours and pay while maintaining their pension benefits.

Pupil discipline

It is acknowledged that there are already support strategies in place to help schools to deal with difficult pupils; nevertheless, poor pupil behaviour is seen as a source of stress for teachers. All schools have school discipline policies and these should be applied rigorously with immediate support provided where necessary to any teacher experiencing difficulties with discipline.

Technology

Schools are now advanced in terms of technology and this should be utilised where possible to make administrative tasks easier and reduce workload. Teachers also need to be taught how to use any technology to their advantage. Consideration must also be given to the teacher's ability and confidence in using technology. Some one-to-one teaching for staff should be provided when needed.

Health and well-being policy

A model health and well-being policy should be developed by the Teacher Health and Well-being Strategy Implementation Group. Time can also be given at staff meetings for the group to talk to staff but also for the staff to actively engage in some well-being exercises such as yoga.

Professional and personal development

Meaningful professional and/or personal development can have a positive impact upon teachers' health and well-being. Progress should be made in setting up a comprehensive programme of continuing professional development. Teachers participating in courses should be provided with sufficient time to follow their agreed course of study.

It is acknowledged that on occasion teachers will opt to study a topic of their own choice rather than those identified by the school. It is recommended that schools be encouraged to allow flexibility in the interests of the teacher's well-being and, where possible, support the teacher in engaging in personal development.

Communications

One of the most common causes of friction in organisations is the lack of effective channels of communication. This, in turn, can lead to misunderstandings and difficulties between members of staff.

Schools should examine their current systems, ensuring that there is input from all staff, with a view to putting in place effective communications systems that are open and transparent.

Impact of pupil mental health issues on teachers

There is a growing awareness of the extent of mental health issues affecting pupils and the impact dealing with these issues may have on teachers. Teachers should be trained to identify the symptoms of pupils suffering from mental health problems and be aware of the reporting procedures so that pupils can access the appropriate help.

Health and safety risk assessment

All teachers carrying out risk assessments should be fully trained in this process. All actions identified through risk assessments should be implemented in full.

Review of health and well-being

Teacher health and well-being can be measured on a regular basis to monitor overall levels but also to track improvement based around programmes that have been introduced into a school. An independent review can be conducted every three years to gain a more detailed evaluation of staff health.

If schools do not look after teachers it is very hard for teachers to work with and help students with challenging behaviours to a level they often need. Teachers must be cared for, and even more so when working with challenging students. A school with teachers who feel supported is more likely to be able to cope with the day-to-day challenging behaviours as the teachers have the knowledge, energy and resources to be able to do so.

I am a big advocate for the well-being of teachers and I hope the ideas described above can be implemented in your working environment. In Chapter 9, I will look at methods to try to reduce the confusion for schools, teachers and parents in relation to the amount of legislation relating to the education of students. Unfortunately, this is not an area that teachers have a big say in. However, I think it is important that schools, teachers and parents are given a voice and listened to when policies are made that relate to teaching methodologies and education.

Clear procedures and policies relating to managing challenging behaviours in schools

Finally, and very importantly, the last message of my book is to the policy makers in education. It is very clear to me that teachers, school administrators, parents and students are confused as to the procedures governing schools in regard to managing challenging behaviours and also as to the availability of resources. I would ask policy makers to do the following:

- Go and spend more time in classrooms where there are challenging behaviours to gain a clear understanding of what it is like to be a teacher.
- Talk more to parents who have children with challenging behaviours.
- Talk more to teachers and listen to their ideas in management techniques, procedures and policies.
- Provide more opportunity for teacher training.
- Look at classroom structures, rooms and staffing to assist in the management of students with challenging behaviours.
- Set up classrooms and or schools specifically for students who have challenging behaviours.
- Create a very clear flow chart of action that teachers and schools can follow when managing students who have challenging behaviours. This process should take into account but override all of the existing legislation in the management of students who have challenging behaviours but also allows for parents to have some choices in how best to educate their child.

This is not easy and will take some time and effort but it needs to be done for the benefit of all involved in education. I would like to see less talking, less meetings, better policy development and more action-based interventions. Education is the right of all children and I believe we need to review our processes in schools to ensure all children receive an education that caters for their individual needs while having consideration for the needs of all students.

10 | Where to from here?

Thank you for taking the time to read this book and I wish you well in working with students who have challenging behaviours. Thank you for taking on the challenge. On more than one occasion I have had former students approach me in their early twenties and thank me for supporting them while at school. My favourite story is as follows:

Catherine was in Year 9 (14 years old) and she had been sent to me (school counsellor) due to her behaviour in art. Catherine stormed in and sat making no eye contact. As per usual I started to ask Catherine about her day, what had happened etc. No response. Thinking quickly I produced the movie Good Will Hunting *and skipped straight to the scene where the counsellor, Robin Williams, sat for an hour in silence with the client, Matt Damon, and nothing was said. Catherine looked at the scene and at the end I explained to Catherine that if she ever needed to talk to me about anything I was always here to help.*

Six years later I bumped into Catherine waiting for a plane at the airport. Catherine asked me if I remembered the time she was in my office to which I replied, 'How could I ever forget it?' Catherine smiled and said, 'Mr Dansie, I was that close to talking to you but I was too angry.' Catherine went on to say, 'The most important thing was, on that day I learnt that there were teachers who cared about me and that made a big difference in my education and attitude to school.'

To me this is what teaching is all about. Catherine epitomises a student who was challenging in her behaviours but who was able to successfully navigate her way through school because she knew that her teachers cared about her.

Typically when working in schools I ask the question for a student who has challenging behaviours: 'What does success look like?' This is a hard question, but to me, success is having students who have an enthusiasm for learning, want to come to school every day and who leave school able to move into a vocation which is of interest to them and in which they are capable of working.

As teachers, success is not always evident as students move on and into different classes and different schools, but they do remember, as we do, the teachers and people who were in their learning.

Please feel free to contact me at tdpsych@bigpond.com as I am always willing to visit schools and work with staff, students and parents. I hope to meet you one day so I can thank you for reading my book but also for making a difference in a student's education.

Cheers

Tim Dansie

Appendix 1

Solutions for James

- Limit time on computer at home by reducing access to wi-fi.
- Remove the computer from his bedroom.
- James can study in the kitchen/dining room where he can be seen.
- Set up a study timetable with clear homework times and fun computing times.
- Teach James to use voice-activated software to get written work done faster.
- James's teachers can monitor progress with assignment work.
- Reduce the amount of written work James needs to do.
- James could do verbal assessments rather than written assessments.
- James could attend after-school homework club.
- James could talk to teachers about subject content he finds challenging.
- James could complete some career guidance/planning for life after school.
- James could have a mentor at school who he talks to if struggling to keep up with work.

Appendix 2

How to engage parents in schools

Having parents actively involved in a school can be a double-edged sword as sometimes the parents can, in fact, create more problems. However, on most occasions and through my experiences I think that involving parents in a school is very beneficial, but an ongoing challenge for schools is how to most effectively involve them.

Here are some ways to get parents working with us in schools:

- Invite parents into the school and classroom on a regular basis.
- Use name tags for parents on all occasions so staff and other parents can learn names.
- Provide parents with a map of the school so they know where to go.
- Have students present to talk to parents and direct them through the school.
- Give parents training in specific areas where they can help.
- Communicate to parents through a variety of means – for example, students, internet, newsletters and emails.
- Give parents tasks to do that help the students and school community.
- Hold appreciation days for parents.
- Use the expertise of parents to help learning and the presentation of the curriculum. The best outcome I ever had was a parent who was a fire fighter. My students loved the visit to the fire station more than anything else in the year.
- Invite parents on school camps and excursions.

When we have parents supporting our schools, the overall outcomes are better for teachers and students alike. We must not be afraid of asking our parents to help.

Appendix 3

Checklists for identifying behaviours and simple strategies to help in the classroom

The following is a list of checklists and strategies that can be used to help teachers and school staff gain a better understanding of why a student is behaving in the manner they do. The checklists are not a diagnostic tool but they can be used as a guide for teachers and schools. Parents can also be asked to complete checklists as this often creates an awareness for parents of the type of behaviours schools are observing of their child.

In regard to the strategies suggested, I still recommend that teachers and schools refer to professionals and school counsellors to work with students. However, some of the tips provided can be applied on a day-to-day basis at school. The following are some tips to benefit the entire class and school community:

- Role model positive behaviours and have fun with it.
- Build rapport with students – know your students.
- Understand the cognitive ability of a student and modify tasks so students can achieve success.
- Use both positive and negative consequences but remember positive consequences work much better.
- Correct with kindness.
- Work with external professionals to get more ideas on how to help a student.
- Communicate and work with parents.

The following checklists can be downloaded from www.tdpsych.com from within the Teacher Resources section.

Specific learning disorder checklist

'Specific learning disorder' is now recognised as a single overall term for persistent difficulties in mathematics, reading and written expression.

These difficulties in reading, writing, arithmetic or mathematical reasoning are observed to be well below the average range and significantly interfere with academic achievement, occupational performance or activities of daily living.

NB: This checklist is not a diagnostic tool, but provides information about a student's behaviour. Read the indicators below and make notes in regard to the signs a student is showing. If a number of signs are present, please look to gain further information about the student.

Specific learning disorder with an impairment in reading includes possible weaknesses in:

1   Word reading accuracy.
2   Reading rate or fluency.
3   Reading comprehension.

Reading

- Experiences difficulty distinguishing between similar sounds.
- Shows weak articulation skills and verbal expression.
- Grammar skills are quite weak.
- Unable to follow oral discussion and take notes.
- Difficulty with oral language, uses lots of interjections and hesitations (umm, uh, well…)
- Confuses words and letters.
- Often loses place when reading, requires finger tracking.
- Difficulty when silent reading, needs to mouth words or whisper when reading.
- Doesn't enjoy reading.
- Reading is slow and deliberate.
- Lots of word substitutions, omissions and invented words.
- Cannot skim or scan for pertinent information.
- Cannot re-tell parts of the story, prediction skills are weak.
- Uses vague, imprecise language and has a limited vocabulary.

- Uses poor grammar or misuses words in conversation.
- Mispronounces words frequently.
- Confuses words with others that sound similar or are similar-looking words (e.g. beard/bread).
- Has difficulty rhyming.
- Has difficulty understanding instructions or directions.
- Has difficulty recognising and remembering sight words.
- Confuses or reverses letter order in words (e.g. saw/was).
- Demonstrates poor memory for printed words.
- Has weak comprehension of ideas and themes.
- Has significant trouble learning to read.
- Has trouble naming letters.
- Has problems associating letter and sounds, understanding the difference between sounds in words or blending sounds into words.
- Guesses at unfamiliar words rather than using word analysis skills.
- Reads slowly.
- Substitutes or leaves out words while reading.
- Forgets a lot of words and can't often remember what he/she was going to say.
- Not interested in listening to stories, audio files, songs and a variety of listening activities.
- Doesn't enjoy participating in class discussions and rarely raises his/her hand to respond.

Specific learning disorder with impairment in written expression includes possible weaknesses:

1 Spelling accuracy.
2 Grammar and punctuation accuracy.
3 Clarity or organisation of written expression.

Writing

- Rarely enjoys writing and responds negatively to written activities.
- Experiences difficulty when copying instructions from the board.
- Rarely completes written assignments.
- Expresses ideas in a disorganised way and is difficult to follow.
- Punctuation and grammar is weak and often missing.
- Spelling is weak.

- Letters and/or words are often reversed.
- Demonstrates delays in learning to copy and write.
- Writing is messy and incomplete, with many cross-outs and eraser marks.
- Has difficulty remembering shapes of letters.
- Uses uneven spacing between letters and words, and has trouble staying 'on the line'.
- Spells poorly and inconsistently (e.g. the same word appears differently in other places in the same document).
- Has difficulty proofreading and self-correcting work.
- Has difficulty preparing outlines and organising written assignments.
- Fails to develop ideas in writing, so written work is incomplete and too brief.

Specific learning disorder with impairment in mathematics includes possible deficits in:

1 Number sense.
2 Memorisation of arithmetic facts.
3 Accurate or fluent calculation.
4 Accurate maths reasoning.

Mathematics

- Rarely sequences numbers, equations and formulae appropriately.
- Unable to perform 'mental maths'.
- Computations are usually inaccurate.
- Many careless errors, often chooses the wrong operation.
- Difficulty understanding mathematical concepts.
- Rarely uses mathematical terms appropriately both orally and in written work.
- Does not remember the maths facts.
- Cannot do mathematical word problems.
- Has difficulty with simple counting and one-to-one correspondence between number symbols and items/objects.
- Difficulty mastering number knowledge (e.g. recognition of quantities without counting).

- Has difficulty with learning and memorising basic addition and subtraction facts.
- Has difficulty learning strategic counting principles (e.g. by 2, 5, 10, 100).
- Poorly aligns numbers resulting in computation errors.
- Has difficulty estimating (e.g. quantity, value).
- Has difficulty with comparisons (e.g. less than, greater than).
- Has trouble telling time.
- Has trouble conceptualising the passage of time.
- Has difficulty counting rapidly or making calculations.
- Has trouble learning multiplication tables, formulae and rules.
- Has difficulty interpreting graphs and charts.

Most frequently displayed symptoms of a specific learning disorder:

- Short attention span.
- Poor memory.
- Difficulty following directions.
- Inability to discriminate between/among letters, numerals or sounds.
- Poor reading and/or writing ability.
- Eye–hand coordination problems; poorly coordinated.
- Difficulties with sequencing.
- Disorganisation and other sensory difficulties.

Other characteristics that may be present:

- Performs differently from day to day.
- Responds inappropriately in many instances.
- Easily distracted.
- Says one thing, means another.
- Difficult to discipline.
- Does not adjust well to change.
- Difficulty listening and remembering.
- Delayed speech development; immature speech.

Strategies to help students who have specific learning difficulties

Please note that strategies will vary depending on the individual student, the support available within a school and the cognitive functioning ability of the student. The strategies suggested are some ideas which can be used in the classroom.

Strategies for students aged between 5 and 9 years

- Give the student special tasks to do that make them feel good about themselves and helping others.
- Provide the student with a signal they can give you if they do not understand what to do.
- Only ask the student to answer when they have their hand up.
- Do not ask the student to read aloud in class, unless they have been able to practise beforehand.
- Allow the student to use learning cues such as a calculator, dictionary or charts to help them.
- Modify expectations of work to allow the student to achieve some success.
- Check understanding of verbal information.
- Provide the student with short achievable tasks, with lots of positive reinforcement upon completion.
- Provide the student with as many opportunities as possible to build self-esteem at school. Allow the student to demonstrate strengths to peers.
- Allow the student to use the computer or iPad for self-directed learning and provide headphones when doing so.
- Ensure any homework tasks are achievable for students.
- Provide visual cues to assist in remembering information.

Strategies for students aged between 9 and 14 years

- Give the student extra time to think about a problem or answer a question (wait time) before requiring a verbal response.
- Show the student how to do something, rather than just telling them.
- Do not give directions while the student is in the middle of performing a task. Wait until you have their full attention.
- Provide lots of visual reinforcements (pictures, maps, charts, graphs).

- When teaching a new concept, illustrate it while giving a verbal explanation.
- Directions need to be visual and verbal – on the board, on paper and spoken.
- Provide charts showing maths facts or a calculator to minimise interference with new learning.
- Read questions and explain requirements to the student if they are unsure of what to do.
- Give the student extra time to respond to questions, particularly during tests and extra time to complete written tests and assignments.
- Increase the student's self-confidence by calling on them when you know they know the answer.
- Ask non-threatening questions which need only a short answer or opinion.
- Allow the student the opportunity to learn using a variety of approaches.
- Do not ask the student to read aloud in front of their peers, unless they have had time to practise beforehand.
- Do not penalise the student for spelling mistakes.
- Ensure that the student is able to complete homework tasks given to them.
- Monitor the student's progress when completing assignment-based work to make sure the student is keeping up with the work.

Strategies for senior school students

- Give the student special tasks to do that make them feel good about themselves and helping others. Community or volunteer work can be incorporated into schooling.
- Provide the student with a signal they can give you if they do not understand what to do.
- Only ask the student to answer when they have their hand up.
- Do not ask the student to read aloud in class, unless they have been able to practise beforehand.
- Allow the student to use learning cues such as a calculator, dictionary or charts to help learning.
- Modify expectations of work to allow the student to achieve some success.
- Check understanding of verbal information.

- Assist in subject selection to ensure the student selects subjects within their cognitive ability level.
- Provide the student with as many opportunities as possible to build self-esteem at school.
- Allow the student to use the computer as often as possible to present work or assist in learning.
- Provide the student as many opportunities as possible to develop life skills that will aid in the transition from school into the workforce or future study.
- Modify learning tasks so the student is able to achieve some success at school.
- Do not place the student in a position where they will be embarrassed about their learning in front of their peers.
- Communicate with parents regarding progress of work and levels of attainment.
- Encourage the student to look at career planning and pathways to follow upon leaving school.

The ADHD checklist

The behaviours must have a significant impact for at least six months in at least two areas of life, such as at home, social settings and school life and must be more frequent or severe than other children of the same age.

NB: This is not a diagnostic tool but provides information about a student's behaviour. Read the indicators below and make notes in regard to the signs a student is showing. If a number of signs are present, please look to gain further information about the student.

Difficulties with inattention:

- Fails to give close attention to details or makes careless mistakes.
- Has difficulty sustaining attention.
- Appears not to listen.
- Struggles to follow through on instructions.
- Has difficulty with organisation.
- Avoids or dislikes tasks requiring sustained mental effort.

- Tends to lose things.
- Appears easily distracted.
- Appears forgetful in daily activities.

Difficulties with hyperactivity or controlling impulsive behaviour:

- Fidgets with hands or feet or squirms in a chair.
- Has difficulty remaining seated.
- Runs about or climbs excessively and shows difficulty engaging in activities quietly.
- Talks excessively.
- Blurts out answers before questions have been completed.
- Shows difficulty waiting or taking turns.
- Interrupts or intrudes upon others.

Combined difficulties with inattention and hyperactive and impulsive behaviours:

- Shows multiple behaviours from both inattentive and hyperactive/ impulsive lists above.

Strategies for students who have difficulty in concentrating

- Monitor proper behaviour frequently and immediately direct the student to an appropriate behaviour.
- Enforce classroom rules consistently.
- Avoid ridicule and criticism. Remember that students with limited concentration have difficulty staying in control.
- Immediately praise any and all good behaviour and performance.
- Change rewards if they are not effective in motivating behavioural change.
- Find alternate ways to encourage students.
- Teach the student to reward himself or herself. Encourage positive self-talk (e.g. 'You did very well remaining in your seat today. How do you feel about that?'). This encourages the student to think positively about him or herself.
- Reduce the amount of materials present during activities by having the student put away unnecessary items. Have a special place for tools, materials and books.

- Reward more than you punish.
- Try to be patient.
- Place these students up front with their backs to the rest of the class to keep other students out of view.
- Surround students with good peer models, preferably students whom the student views as significant peers.
- Encourage peer tutoring and talkative/collaborative learning.
- A class that has a low student–teacher ratio will be helpful.
- Avoid all distracting stimuli. Try not to place students near air conditioners, high traffic areas, heaters, doors, windows etc.
- Encourage parents to set up appropriate study space at home, with set times and routines established for study. Also, use this home area for parental review of completed homework and organisation.
- Have pre-established consequences for misbehaviour, remain calm, state the infraction of the rule, and avoid debating or arguing with the student.
- Maintain eye contact during verbal instructions.
- Make directions clear and concise. Be consistent with all daily instructions.
- When you ask a student a question, first say the student's name and then pause for a few seconds as a signal for him/her to pay attention.
- To help with changes in assignments, provide clear and consistent transitions between activities and notify the student a few minutes before changing activities.
- Repeat instructions in a calm, positive manner.
- Students may need both verbal and visual directions. You can do this by providing the student with a model of what he/she should be doing.
- You can give a student confidence by starting each assignment with a few questions or activities you know the student can successfully accomplish.
- Self-monitoring techniques can prove effective in the school setting. Self-monitoring of attention involves cueing the student so that he/she can determine how well he is attending to the task at hand. Cueing is often done by providing an audio tone.
- Behaviour management techniques must often be used in the school. By examining a child's specific problem behaviour, understanding its

antecedents and consequences, educators can help students develop behaviours that lead to academic and social success.

- Develop an individualised education programme. By identifying each student's individual strengths and specific learning needs, you can design a plan for mobilising those strengths to improve the student's academic and social performance.
- Gradually reduce the amount of assistance, but keep in mind that these students will need more help for a longer period of time than the student without a disability.
- Require a daily assignment notebook as necessary and make sure each student correctly writes down all assignments. If a student is not capable of this, the teacher should help the student.
- Initial the notebook daily to signify completion of homework assignments. (Parents should also sign.)
- Use the notebook for daily communication with parents.
- Consider alternative activities/exercises that can be utilised with less difficulty for the student, but have the same or similar learning objectives.
- You can give a student confidence by starting each lab assignment with a few questions or activities you know the student can successfully accomplish.
- Make sure all students comprehend the instructions before beginning their tasks.
- Simplify complex directions. Avoid multiple commands.
- Repeat instructions in a calm, positive manner.
- Help the students feel comfortable with seeking assistance (most students will not ask for help).
- Assign only one task at a time.
- Modify assignments as needed for the student.
- Keep in mind that students with ADHD are easily frustrated and they need assurance of things that are common in science, e.g. when an experiment does not turn out as expected. Stress, pressure and fatigue can help reduce their self-control and can lead to poor behaviour.
- Provide additional reading time and shorten the amount of required reading.
- Avoid oral reading.
- For all assignments, clearly identify expectations in writing.

- Make required book lists available prior to the first day of class to allow students to begin their reading early or arrange access to the audio books.
- Encourage the use of audio books to support students' reading assignments.
- Provide students with chapter outlines, or handouts that highlight key points in their readings.
- Read aloud material written on the board or that is presented in handouts or transparencies.
- Provide the student with published book summaries, synopses or digests of major reading assignments to review beforehand. Downloads for Cliffs Notes are also available for computer use (and for transformation to audio files).
- Review and discuss with the student the steps involved in a research activity. Think about which step(s) may be difficult for the specific functional limitations of the student and with the student devise ways to accommodate that student.
- Consider alternative activities/exercises that can be utilised with less difficulty for the student, but has the same or similar learning objectives.
- Repeat instructions in a calm, positive manner.
- When giving tests, make sure you are testing knowledge and not attention span.
- Give extra time and frequent breaks for certain challenging examination tasks (e.g. maths related). Students with limited concentration may work slowly.
- Testing aids such as: 1) use of a highlighter; 2) computer with/without spell check/grammar/cut and paste features; and 3) suitable setting such as private room and preferential seating.

Autism spectrum disorder checklist

A child must have had symptoms from early childhood, even if these are not recognised until later. These symptoms cause significant impairment in social, occupational or other important areas of functioning.

NB: This is not a diagnostic tool but provides information about a student's behaviour. Read the indicators below and make notes in regard to the signs a student is showing. If a number of signs are present, please look to gain further information about the student.

Sensory issues:

- Shows unusual reactions to the way things sound (vacuum cleaner, loud noises), smell, taste, look or feel.
- Is extremely sensitive to sensory experiences – for example, is easily upset by certain sounds, or will eat only foods with a certain texture.
- Likes to rub fingers on certain objects repetitively for feel.
- Seeks sensory stimulation, such as having back rubbed.

Fixated interests and repetitive behaviours:

- Has a tendency to flap their hands, rock their body, back-arching, walking on their toes or spinning in circles.
- Inflexible and insists on sticking to routines, getting upset by minor changes.
- Likes things in a certain order, for example all the same colour or same size.
- Lines up toys or other objects.
- Plays with toys the same way every time.
- Likes parts of objects (e.g. wheels).
- Is easily upset by change and must follow routines – for example, sleeping, feeding or leaving the house must be done in the same way every time.
- Has an intense interest in certain objects and becomes 'stuck' on particular toys or objects – for example, flicking the light switch off and on repeatedly, or plays only with cars.
- Is very interested in unusual objects or activities – for example, trains, metal objects or watching a specific ad on TV.
- Can get very emotional and act with frustration and aggression if something unexpected happens.

Social communication skills:

- Prefers to play alone and has few if any friends.
- Finds it difficult to read social situations.

- Seems unaware or disinterested in peer group pressure.
- Has flat or inappropriate facial expressions not reflective of the social circumstance.
- Does not understand personal space boundaries.
- Difficulty reading facial expressions and body language.
- Avoids or resists physical contact and tries to avoid eye contact.
- Is not comforted by others during distress.
- Has trouble understanding other people's feelings or talking about own feelings.
- Repeats words or phrases over and over.
- Gives unrelated answers to questions.
- Makes inappropriate comments or does socially inappropriate things.
- Does not initiate or join in games with other children.
- Does not understand the moral in stories or films.
- Asks for explicit information about others' feelings, for example asking, 'Are you angry at me?'
- Sees things from his/her own point of view and expects others to read their mind.
- Has difficulty communicating needs and wants.
- Lacks entry point strategies with people who are new to them.
- Uses few or no gestures (e.g. does not wave goodbye).
- Does not understand jokes, sarcasm or teasing.

Some people with ASD have other symptoms which include:

- Hyperactivity (very active).
- Impulsivity (acting without thinking).
- Short attention span.
- Aggression.
- Causing self-injury.
- Temper tantrums.
- Unusual eating and sleeping habits.
- Unusual mood or emotional reactions.
- Lack of fear or more fear than expected.

Disruptive externalising behaviours are immediately apparent in the classroom or at home and may include task refusal, verbal or physical aggression or self-injury. Internalising behaviours such as anxiety, obsessive thoughts, perfectionism and problems with changes or unmet expectations may not be as observable.

Write down your own observations of the child that best illustrate their typical behaviour or history of behaviours, if any.

For example, 'Tim always loved Thomas the tank engine as a boy, now this has been replaced by the Avengers.'

Strategies to help ASD students

The strategies used to help a student with ASD will vary significantly based on the severity of the condition. The strategies below are aimed at younger students with ASD.

Strategies for junior school students

- Use task analysis – very specific tasks in sequential order.
- Always keep language simple and concrete. Get the point across in as few words as possible. Typically, it's far more effective to say, 'Pens down, close your book and line up to go outside' than 'It looks so nice outside. Let's do our science lesson now. As soon as you've finished your writing, close your books and line up at the door. We're going to study plants outdoors today.'
- Teach specific social rules/skills, such as turn taking and social distance.
- Give fewer choices. If the student is asked to pick a colour, say red, only give him two to three choices to pick from. The more choices, the more confused the student will become.
- If you ask a question or give an instruction and are greeted with a blank stare, reword your sentence. Asking the student what you just said helps clarify that you have been understood.
- Avoid using sarcasm. If the student accidentally knocks all your papers on the floor and you say 'Great!' you will be taken literally and this action might be repeated on a regular basis.
- Avoid using idioms. 'Put your thinking caps on', 'Open your ears' and 'Zip your lips' will leave the student completely mystified and wondering how to do that.

- Give very clear choices and try not to leave choices open ended. You're bound to get a better result by asking 'Do you want to read or draw?' than by asking 'What do you want to do now?'
- Repeat instructions and check understanding. Using short sentences ensures clarity of instructions.
- Provide a very clear structure and a set daily routine, including time for play.
- Teach what 'finished' means and help the student to identify when something has finished and something different has started. Take a photo of what you want the finished product to look like and show the student. If you want the room cleaned up, take a picture of how you want it to look when it is clean. The student can use this for a reference.
- Providing warning of any impending change of routine, or switch of activity.
- Address the student individually at all times (for example, the student may not realise that an instruction given to the whole class also includes him).
- Calling the student's name and saying, 'I need you to listen to this, as this is something for you to do.'
- Using various means of presentation – visual, physical guidance, peer modelling etc.
- Recognising that some change in manner or behaviour may reflect anxiety (which may be triggered by a [minor] change to routine).
- Do not take apparently rude or aggressive behaviour personally. Recognise that the target for the student's anger may be unrelated to the source of that anger.
- Avoid overstimulation. Minimise or remove distracters or provide access to an individual work area or booth when a task involving concentration is set. Colourful wall displays can be distracting for the student and he may find noise very difficult to cope with.
- Seek to link work to the student's particular interests.
- Explore word-processing and computer-based learning for literacy.
- Protect the student from teasing at free times and provide peers with some awareness of the student's particular needs if required.

- Allow the student to avoid certain activities (such as sports and games) which they may not understand or like; and support the student in open-ended and group tasks.
- Allow some access to obsessive behaviour as a reward for positive efforts.

Recommendations for ASD students in middle school and high school

The following recommendations address some of the issues an older ASD student faces on a daily basis.

Social interactions:

- Protect the student from bullying and teasing at school. Students must be made aware that the student has different interests and abilities and that it is okay to be this way.
- Emphasise the proficient academic skills of the student by creating cooperative learning situations in which talents and skills will be viewed as an asset by peers, thereby engendering acceptance.
- The student might benefit from a 'buddy system'. The student's teacher can educate a sensitive classmate about the student's situation and seat them next to each other.
- The student is likely to be somewhat reclusive, thus the student's teacher must foster involvement with others.
- The student's interactions with his peers can be observed and then his teachers can talk to the student about what is and is not appropriate behaviour.

Poor concentration:

- A tremendous amount of regimented external structure must be provided for the student to be productive in the classroom. Assignments should be broken down into small units and frequent teacher feedback and redirection should be offered.
- The student will benefit from timed work sessions. This will help the student to organise themselves. Classwork that is not completed within the time limit (or that is done carelessly within the time limit) must be made up during the student's own time (i.e. during break or during the time used for pursuit of special interests). The student may be stubborn; he needs firm expectations and a

structured programme that teaches him that compliance with the rules leads to positive reinforcement (this kind of programme will motivate the student to be productive, thus enhancing self-esteem and lowering stress levels).

- As the student can have difficulty with concentration, slow clerical speed and organisation, it may be necessary to lessen his homework/ classwork load and/or provide time in a resource room where a support teacher can provide the additional structure the student needs to complete any work.
- Seat the student at the front of the class and direct frequent questions to him or her to help the student to attend to the lesson.
- Work out a non-verbal signal with the student (e.g. a gentle pat on the shoulder) for times when they are not attending.

Poor motor coordination:

- When assigning timed units of work, make sure the student's writing speed is taken into account.
- The student may need more time than peers to complete exams. (Taking exams in a different room not only offers more time, but would also provide the added structure and teacher redirection the student needs to focus on the task at hand.)

Academic difficulties:

- Provide a highly individualised academic programme engineered to offer consistent successes. The student needs great motivation to not follow their own impulses. Learning must be rewarding and not anxiety provoking.
- Do not assume that the student will understand something just because they parrot back what they have heard.
- Offer added explanation and try to simplify when lesson concepts are abstract.
- Emotional nuances, multiple levels of meaning and relationship issues as presented in novels will often not be understood.
- Academic work may be of poor quality because the student is not motivated to exert effort in areas in which they are not interested. Very firm expectations must be set for the quality of work produced. Work executed within timed periods must not only be

complete, but done carefully. The student should be expected to correct poorly executed classwork during break or during the time they usually pursue their own interests.

Social (pragmatic) communication disorder checklist

Social (pragmatic) communication disorder is characterised by persistent difficulty with the use of social language and communication skills.

NB: This is not a diagnostic tool but provides information about a student's behaviour. Read the indicators below and make notes in regard to the signs a student is showing. If a number of signs are present, please look to gain further information about the student.

Poor social skills:

- Has difficulty greeting peers and sharing information in an appropriate manner for the social context.
- Shows persistent difficulties taking turns in conversation.
- Talks non-stop regardless of whether the listener is interested or not.
- Has difficulty sorting out conflicts.
- Struggles to maintain friendships.

Difficulties understanding and adapting socially appropriate behaviour:

- Speaks distinctively, has an unusual intonation or speaks with a loud monotone voice.
- Shows too little or too much eye contact.
- Does not know how to use verbal and non-verbal signals to manage social interactions.
- Has difficulty rephrasing when misunderstood.

Difficulties with non-verbal communication:

- Has persistent difficulties with non-verbal communication.
- Does not seem to understand facial expression or gestures.
- Stands too close to others or is 'wooden' when cuddled.

Difficulties making inferences and understanding idioms:

- Takes things very literally.
- Has difficulty making inferences.
- Reads very accurately but comprehension of what is read is poor.
- Has difficulty recounting.
- Finds it difficult to mime or to mimic others.
- Delayed academic progress resulting from difficulties in communication.

Strategies to help students with social pragmatic disorder

- Role model positive social behaviours in the classroom.
- Teach the student how to give and receive greetings.
- Provide opportunities for games where students need to take turns and there is a winner and a loser.
- Role model winning and losing behaviours.
- Teach appropriate body language to use in situations but also how to read and understand body language of others.
- Provide students opportunities to initiate conversations with peers.
- Show students how to give and receive compliments.
- Teach students how to ask for help when needed.
- Teach strategies in how to manage anger.
- Teach students how to compromise with peers.
- Provide the opportunity for interactions in the classroom as often as possible.
- Correct with kindness when things don't go to plan.
- Have hand signals to use for a student when in a social situation to remind them of a skill, e.g. a thumbs up to reinforce taking turns and listening.
- Work with parents to reinforce skills at home.
- Look at social skills training programmes at school for students who need support external to the classroom environment.

The generalised anxiety disorder checklist

Children with generalised anxiety disorder (GAD) experience excessive anxiety and worry, occurring more days than not for at least six months, concerning a number of events. These symptoms are excessive, intrusive, persistent and debilitating.

NB: This is not a diagnostic tool but provides information about a student's behaviour. Read the indicators below and make notes in regard to the signs a student is showing. If a number of signs are present, please look to gain further information about the student.

Difficulties with controlling worries:

- Has unreasonable worries about things before they happen.
- Has many worries about friends, school or activities that occur more days than not.
- Shows an inability to control worry.
- Ruminating, resulting in making events feel bigger than they may be.
- The potential to focus on the negative side of things and imagining the worst.
- Excessive worry about a change in routine.
- Fears of meeting or talking to people.
- Rigidity and inflexibility, self-criticism, guilty thoughts etc.
- Difficulties with restlessness and being on edge.
- The need for clarification and the potential for excessive questioning.
- Experiences constant thoughts and fears about safety of self or family members.
- Need for affirmation.
- Inability to relax and restlessness.
- Clingy behaviour with family members.
- Restlessness, irritability, tantrums.
- Avoidance behaviours, such as avoiding things or places or refusing to do things or go places.

Fatigue:

- Muscle aches or tension.
- Is easily tired.
- Sleep difficulties such as having trouble falling asleep, or restless and unsatisfying sleep.
- Frequent stomach aches, headaches or other physical complaints.
- Refusing to go to school.

- Crying.
- Appears sad or depressed.
- Feelings of loneliness.

Difficulties with concentration:

- Shows a lack of concentration and motivation.
- Disinterested.
- Perfectionism and procrastination.
- Poor memory.
- Demonstrates fears of embarrassment or making mistakes.
- Shows a low self-esteem and lack of self-confidence.
- Fatigue.

Irritability:

- Being easily startled.
- Irritability and hypervigilance.
- Unwillingness to engage in unfamiliar situations.
- Feeling as though there is a lump in the throat.
- Opposition and defiance.

Strategies to help students with generalised anxiety disorder

- Role model problem-solving behaviours to students where possible.
- Teach students to use a scale from 0–10 to rate their level of anxiety.
- Provide a variety of means for the student to communicate that they are anxious. Students need to learn to communicate how they are feeling so teachers can then help.
- Encourage the student to think of ways to reduce their levels of anxiety. Provide strategies if the student is unable to think of ideas.
- Use hand signals so the student can communicate their levels of anxiety.
- Have strategies in place that can be used to make the student feel safe (place to go when feeling anxious).
- Identify situations that can increase anxiety (specific subject or place in the school) and develop strategies to reduce anxiety levels based on the situation.
- Communicate with other staff members so staff know that a student may be anxious within their class.

- Teach students how to do deep breathing as a form of relaxation when anxious.
- Use lots of positive reinforcement to make a student feel confident in the classroom.
- Provide as many opportunities as possible to build the self-esteem of a student.
- Role model that it is okay for people to make mistakes.
- Communicate with parents so strategies can be adopted at home and at school.
- Set up consistent class routines so students know what to prepare for each day.

The conduct disorder checklist

Conduct disorder is characterised by four primary behaviours. At least three symptoms must be present in the past 12 months with one symptom having been present in the past six months. The symptoms must cause significant impairment in at least two areas of life such as at home, social settings and school life, and must be more frequent or severe than other children of the same age. Children may also display limited empathy and little concern for the feelings, wishes and well-being of others.

NB: This is not a diagnostic tool but provides information about a student's behaviour. Read the indicators below and make notes in regard to the signs a student is showing. If a number of signs are present, please look to gain further information about the student.

Aggression to people and animals:

- Bullies, threatens or intimidates others.
- Often initiates physical fights.
- Has used a weapon that could cause serious physical harm to others (e.g. a bat, brick, broken bottle, knife or gun).
- Is physically cruel to people or animals.
- Steals from a victim while confronting them (e.g. assault).
- Forces someone into sexual activity.
- Often angry and uncooperative.

Destruction of property:

- Has deliberately engaged in fire setting with the intention to cause damage.
- Deliberately damages or destroys other's property or possessions (e.g. graffiti, breaking objects).

Deceitfulness, lying or stealing:

- Lies to obtain goods or favours or to avoid obligations.
- Is deceitful or invents or exaggerates stories about themselves.
- Steals items from shops, school or other premises without confronting the victim.
- Steals from family or friends.
- Blames others and does not accept responsibility.
- Has broken into someone else's building, house or car.
- Incriminates others for his or her own advantage.

Serious violations of rules:

- Is often out at night despite parental objections.
- Runs away from home.
- Often truant from school.
- Uses illegal drugs.
- Drinks excessive alcohol or smokes under age.

Strategies to help a student with conduct disorder

- Modify all school work so the student can achieve success.
- Allow the student to attend lessons where they feel that they can control their behaviour.
- Teach strategies to keep calm when becoming frustrated.
- Use hand signals for positive reinforcement of behaviours but also as a means of asking a student to reduce a negative behaviour.
- Establish a mentor for the student to work with as needed.
- Encourage the student in sporting or community activities.
- Provide the student opportunities to help other students – older students could read to younger students, set up activities for teachers or complete tasks around the school to benefit the school community.

- Use consequences when necessary but only after a student has calmed down. The consequences should be meaningful and short.
- Ensure the student understands why the consequences are in place.
- Find an interest of the student and build rapport based on the interest.
- Work on changing one behaviour at a time.
- Use a whole-school approach to being positive towards the student.
- Teach cues such as NPC which stands for 'no physical contact' to use at break or lunchtime. A student may need a sensory cue such as a band aid on their finger to remind them of NPC.
- Work with parents to modify one behaviour at a time. Parent support may be needed.

Depression checklist

Children with depression may have difficulties organising and motivating themselves, maintaining friendships and managing everyday activities. These can impact all areas of life, at home, in social settings and school life. Depression is defined when more than five symptoms are present during a two-week period.

NB: This is not a diagnostic tool but provides information about a student's behaviour. Read the indicators below and make notes in regard to the signs a student is showing. If a number of signs are present, please look to gain further information about the student.

Socialisation activities:

- Social withdrawal and wanting to be alone most of the time.
- Having difficulty getting along with others.
- Not wanting to go to school.
- Not enjoying everyday activities.
- Increased sensitivity to rejection.
- Restlessness and agitation.
- Vocal outbursts or crying.
- Increased anger and hostility, displaying irritable behaviour.

Loss of interest in school and poor academic performance:

- Increased difficulty concentrating and indecisiveness.
- Reduced ability to function at home or with friends, in school, extra-curricular activities, and in other hobbies or interests.
- Reduced academic performance.
- Loss of interest.
- Concentration difficulties and impaired thinking.
- Difficulty making decisions.
- Difficulty completing school work.
- Frequent absenteeism.

A change in appearance:

- Fatigue and lack of energy.
- Weight or appetite change.
- Headaches.
- Stomach aches.
- Joint or back aches.
- Changes in sleeping quality, e.g. sleeplessness or excessive sleep.
- Persistent sad or irritable mood.
- Feelings of guilt, worthlessness, hopelessness, emptiness and sadness.

Warning signs of suicidal behaviour in children include:

- Many depressive symptoms (changes in eating, sleeping, activities).
- Social isolation, including isolation from the family.
- Talk of suicide, hopelessness or helplessness.
- Increased acting out of undesirable behaviours (sexual/behavioural).
- Increased risk-taking behaviours.
- Frequent accidents.
- Substance abuse.
- Focus on morbid and negative themes.
- Talk about death and dying.
- Increased crying or reduced emotional expression.
- Giving away possessions.

Strategies to help a student with depression

- Build rapport and talk about the student's interests with them.
- Always smile and greet the student when you see them.
- Provide lots of positive reinforcement.
- Use humour and have a laugh with the student (ideally based on their interests).
- Encourage the student to keep up with academic demands, but modify if needed.
- If depression is severe, consider how many subjects the student can complete. If necessary, focus on the core subjects.
- Provide opportunities for the student to have fun at school.
- Teach the student to monitor and communicate how they are feeling in your class. Ask the student, 'Is there anything I can do to help you?'
- Focus on positive behaviours and remind the student of their strengths. Ask the student what it was that made them happy during a lesson if they were observed smiling.
- Encourage the student to be active – sport or community activities.
- Encourage the student to build positive friendships.
- Provide the student an opportunity to help others – could be a peer mentor for younger students.
- Have regular discussions with the student/parents/school counsellor/outside professional about the progress of the student and about what you can do to help.

Developmental coordination disorder checklist

Developmental coordination disorder is a term used to describe children who show substantial difficulty with motor coordination that significantly and persistently interferes with everyday tasks and has an impact on academic achievement and social well-being.

NB: This is not a diagnostic tool but provides information about a student's behaviour. Read the indicators below and make notes in regard to the signs a student is showing. If a number of signs are present, please look to gain further information about the student.

History of early developmental symptoms:

- Clumsiness.
- Delays in sitting up, crawling and walking.
- Problems with sucking and swallowing during first year of life.
- Problems with gross motor coordination (for example, jumping, hopping or standing on one foot).
- Problems with visual or fine motor coordination (for example, writing, using scissors, tying shoelaces, or tapping one finger to another).
- Difficulties drinking water from a drink bottle.

Motor skills difficulties:

- Motor skills that are below peers of the same age and are not considered part of a neurologic condition or visual impairment affecting movement (e.g. cerebral palsy, muscular dystrophy or a degenerative disorder).
- Displays clumsiness (e.g. dropping or bumping into objects).
- Slowness and inaccuracy of performance of motor skills (e.g. catching an object).
- Has difficulty using scissors (e.g. cutting out a circle).
- Shows difficulty riding a bike, or participating in sports.
- Has slumped posture.
- Holds their head in their hands.
- Leans on others.
- Shows a tendency to lie down, wiggles or falls over.
- Has frequent problems writing letters and doing sums.
- Shows handwriting that is slow and untidy, complaining of discomfort in the shoulder and hand.
- Shows a speed–accuracy trade-off (very slow with good legibility or very fast with poor legibility).
- Has an awkward pencil grasp.
- Produces less work than peers and shows frustration with its quality.
- Has a lot of eraser marks.
- Has poor organisation of space on the page.
- Shows avoidance behaviours, including refusal to participate or rushing through the task.

- Has difficulty with subjects that require handwriting, including maths, spelling and written language.
- Has difficulty copying from the board, making frequent errors and omissions.
- Demonstrates a dislike for writing, complaining that it is boring.
- Shows consistent difficulty colouring pictures, tracing designs or making figures from clay.
- Has difficulty building with construction toys.
- Has difficulty organising their desk, locker, school bag, items to bring home from school and the writing on their page.

Children with DCD frequently have co-occurring developmental difficulties which impact on their everyday function and capacity for learning. These may include:

- Attention difficulties: these may be related to anxiety and poor emotional self-regulation.
- Poor working memory which makes it difficult for the child to remember instructions and keep a goal in mind.
- Specific language impairment.
- Joint hypermobility and associated weakness with low muscle tone and poor levels of fitness.

Strategies to help a student with developmental coordination disorder

- Consider how desks are placed within a classroom. Easy movement between desks helps the student with DCD.
- Encourage a neat desk without clutter.
- Reduce writing tasks.
- Use one writing book for all subjects and one for homework – less books to carry for marking but also easier for a student to organise.
- Do colouring in or dot-to-dot activities for younger children.
- Allow the use of a computer to type up large amounts of work.
- Teach the student coordination activities such as juggling.
- Do balance activities or yoga as a quick break during lessons.
- Play Wii Fit – balance activities and lots of fun.
- Focus on the student's strengths – this may mean oral assessments at times rather than just written assessments.

- Be mindful if doing fitness or PE that the student is likely to find many of the tasks difficult. Be conscious of not embarrassing the student in front of peers.

Impulse control disorder checklist

People with impulse control disorder cannot resist the urge to do something harmful to themselves or others. Impulse Control Disorders include addictions to alcohol or drugs, eating disorders, compulsive gambling, and behaviours involving non-human objects, suffering, humiliation, compulsive hair pulling, stealing, fire setting and intermittent explosive attacks of rage.

NB: This is not a diagnostic tool but provides information about a student's behaviour. Read the indicators below and make notes in regard to the signs a student is showing. If a number of signs are present, please look to gain further information about the student.

Behavioural difficulties:

- Displays unusual or unnecessary aggressive behaviours.
- Acts out risky behaviours, such as stealing, playing with fire.
- Demonstrates agitation, irritability or difficulty concentrating.
- Shows a lack of patience and endurance.
- Shows more interest in promiscuous or sexualised behaviours.
- Has an excessive fascination with fire or other unusual behaviours.

Physical problems:

- Has burns or apparent injuries, hair loss or unusual bruising resulting from fights, self-injury or playing with fire.

Emotional difficulties:

- Has periods of emotional detachment, depression or increased levels of anxiety.
- Often lies.
- Smokes or takes illegal drugs or binge drinks.

Difficulties with friendships:

- Has few, if any friends.
- Interacts with difficulty in social situations.

Strategies to help a student with impulse control disorder

- Build rapport with the student through learning about their interests.
- Focus on improving behavioural outcomes rather than academic outcomes. The academic progress will come with improved behaviour.
- Modify learning tasks to allow the student success.
- Provide short learning tasks with immediate reinforcement.
- Allow the student an opportunity to burn off energy during class time.
- Provide a buddy for younger students at break and lunchtime to help the student in the yard.
- Teach the rules to games and play with them if needed.
- Teach the student strategies to stop and think. Use sensory or visual cues and positive reinforcement as a means of helping the student to control impulsive behaviours.
- Modify timetable so the student attends lessons where they are able to cope and control behaviour. In non-attending lessons the student can complete self-directed learning or spend time with the school counsellor or behavioural counsellor. In some cases the student will need to be home or away from school.
- Help the student to develop positive friendships. Social skills may need to be taught to the student.
- Encourage the student into positive pursuits at school and within the community.

Internet gaming disorder checklist

Internet gaming disorder is considered to involve persistent and recurrent use of the internet to engage in games, often with other players, leading to significant impairment or distress.

NB: This is not a diagnostic tool but provides information about a student's behaviour. Read the indicators below and make notes in regard to the signs a student is showing. If a number of signs are present, please look to gain further information about the student.

Preoccupation with internet gaming:

- Shows a preoccupation with and continued excessive use of certain games.
- Mirrors certain characteristics of games in their social play.
- Has experienced a loss of interest in other activities.
- Has had unsuccessful attempts to control the excessive behaviour.

Deceiving others regarding the amount of time spent gaming:

- Acts dishonestly.
- Is defensive.

Use of this behaviour to escape or relieve a negative mood:

- Displays euphoric feelings when in front of the computer.
- Is drawn back to the behaviour with high frequency.

Withdrawal symptoms of irritability, anxiety or sadness:

- Displays agitated behaviours when asked to stop playing games on the internet.
- Shows excessive worry or has anxiety.
- Shows feelings of guilt.

Jeopardises school work and socialisation:

- Shows an inability to manage homework and other schedules.
- Has little sense of time.
- Is socially isolated.
- Avoids doing homework.
- Has trouble getting to sleep at night.

Physical difficulties:

- Complains of or experiences backache, wrist, neck or headaches.
- Is chronically tired or acts fatigued with other tasks.
- Experiences blurred or strained vision.

Strategies to help a student with internet gaming disorder

- Allow the student to complete some homework tasks at school at break, lunchtime or after school.
- Set homework tasks that do not require the use of the internet.
- Monitor internet use of students in lessons.
- Help the student set up a weekly plan that incorporates a good life balance.
- Learn how to use the internet well yourself so you know if students are hiding screens in lessons.
- Reward students with the use of free internet time when work is completed.
- Encourage students into community or sporting activities at school.
- Help students to develop positive friendships at school so they have students to study or spend time with at weekends.
- Encourage the use of computers for the good of the class or school community. A student could do computer-based tasks for other students or staff.
- Talk to parents and provide strategies on how they can help their child.

Oppositional defiant disorder (ODD) checklist

Oppositional defiant disorder (ODD) is a recurrent pattern of negative, defiant, disobedient and hostile behaviour toward authority figures that persists for at least six months, and where the child shows frequent occurrence of at least four behaviours that is shown more often than is typical for their peers.

NB: This is not a diagnostic tool but provides information about a student's behaviour. Read the indicators below and make notes in regard to the signs a student is showing. If a number of signs are present, please look to gain further information about the student.

Angry and irritable mood:

- Often loses temper.
- Is often touchy or easily annoyed by others.
- Is often angry and resentful.

Argumentative and defiant behaviour:

- Often argues with adults or people in authority.
- Often actively defies or refuses to comply with adults' requests or rules.
- Often deliberately annoys people.
- Often blames others for his or her mistakes or misbehaviour.

Vindictiveness:

- Is often spiteful or vindictive.
- Has shown spiteful or vindictive behaviour at least twice in the past six months.

Mild: Symptoms occur only in one setting, such as only at home, school, work or with peers.
Moderate: Some symptoms occur in at least two settings.
Severe: Some symptoms occur in three or more settings.

Strategies to help a student with oppositional defiance disorder

- Look for patterns in behaviour to allow better prediction of when defiant behaviours will occur.
- Teach the student to recognise how they are feeling when entering the classroom at the start of the day, after break, after lunch and when moving between classes. If a student is feeling frustrated, alternative activities can be implemented to allow the student to calm themselves.
- Teach the student how to communicate why it is they are feeling angry/defiant.
- Have a mentor the student can talk to if feeling very angry/defiant. The student can have a hand signal to give teachers alerting them to the need to go and talk to the mentor or even to move to a safe place in the classroom.
- Teach problem-solving strategies to the student.
- Provide positive rewards for good behaviours.
- Provide consequences for inappropriate behaviours, but ensure the student understands why the consequences are in place. This may need to be done when the student has calmed down from their anger.

- Establish consistency in approaches to the student's management between parents and teachers.
- Correct the student in a quiet and caring way when behaviour is inappropriate. Where possible this can be done when peers are not present.
- Do not get drawn into debates and discussions with the student when they want to argue or when they are being defiant.
- Provide the student with the opportunity to mix and play with his peers. Involve the student in clubs and activities that will enable them to enjoy the company of people with similar interests.
- The student needs to perceive school as a place where they can achieve success and feel important. Self-esteem can be raised by providing the opportunity to succeed with learning and by giving specific tasks to do within the classroom that are important to the functioning of the class. Building self-esteem will be of great importance for the student.
- The focus for the defiant student at school should be in the development of positive behaviours as a priority over the learning of literacy and numeracy. This will come as positive behaviours develop.

Post-traumatic stress disorder checklist

Post-traumatic stress disorder (PTSD) in children and adolescents can occur as a result of a child's exposure to one or more major traumatic events. These events can include physical or sexual assault, emotional abuse or neglect, natural disasters, accidents, traumatic death or injury of a loved one.

NB: This is not a diagnostic tool but provides information about a student's behaviour. Read the indicators below and make notes in regard to the signs a student is showing. If a number of signs are present, please look to gain further information about the student.

Re-experiences of the traumatic event:

- Re-enactment of event/s through play, stories or drawings, unusual, inappropriate themes in which aspects of the trauma are repeated.
- Has new phobias and anxieties that seem unrelated to the trauma (such as a fear of monsters).

Avoidance of things associated to the trauma experience:

- Spending more time than usual in imaginary places.
- Difficulties with physical contact (in abuse cases).
- Avoidance of distressing memories, thoughts, feelings or external reminders of the event.
- Shows an inability to remember aspects of the event.

Negative thinking and negative mood:

- Shows an increase in protective behaviours towards loved ones.
- Is withdrawing socially from friends and others.
- Is disinterested in activities that were previously enjoyed.
- Shows a loss of previously learned skills and abilities.
- Has developed irritability, is on edge and shows aggressive or reckless behaviour.

Physical responses to re-experiencing the event or negative mood:

- Shows fears of being separated from their parent or loved ones.
- Has apparent tiredness and fatigue.
- Complains of aches and pains with no apparent cause.
- Experiences intense physical reactions to reminders of the event (e.g. pounding heart, rapid breathing, nausea, muscle tension, sweating).
- Is tired and reports poor sleep.

Strategies to help a student with post-traumatic stress disorder

- The focus needs to be on making the classroom environment one where the student feels safe.
- Modify all learning tasks so the student can achieve success with learning.
- Sit the student with peers who are kind and friendly.

- Do not put the student on the spot to answer questions or in situations likely to cause embarrassment.
- Establish clear day-to-day routines for the student to learn and settle into.
- Allow the student to only attend lessons within the safe classroom environment if necessary.
- Provide the opportunity for self-directed learning on an iPad or computer.
- Build self-esteem through lots of positive reinforcement.
- Provide activities to do for the student within the classroom that make them feel valued.
- Encourage the student into sport or community activities with peers to build strong friendships.
- Teach the student and class relaxation activities to use if feeling stressed.
- Work closely with the school counsellor or an external professional to seek further advice on how to help the student.

Reactive attachment disorder checklist

Reactive attachment disorder is considered to be a consistent pattern of inhibited, emotionally withdrawn behaviour towards adult caregivers that has been present for more than 12 months.

NB: This is not a diagnostic tool but provides information about a student's behaviour. Read the indicators below and make notes in regard to the signs a student is showing. If a number of signs are present, please look to gain further information about the student.

Emotionally withdrawn:

- Rarely attempts to seek comfort.
- Rarely responds to comfort.
- Displays avoidance or resistance to comforting.
- Is wooden and gives 'stiff' hugs and is not 'cuddly'.
- Shows a lack of guilt or remorse.
- Blames others for their own mistakes.
- Shows no positive response to interactions.

Social or emotional disturbances:

- Has a history of insufficient care, e.g. emotional needs for comfort, stimulation and affection have not been met, or repeated changes of primary caregivers.
- Shows minimal social and emotional responsiveness to others.
- Has episodes of unexplained irritability, sadness or fearfulness with adult caregivers.
- Overly friendly to strangers, but unable to be affectionate with those close to them.
- Has mood swings or temper tantrums.
- Displays regressive behaviours (baby-talk, noisemaking, animal noises, etc.).
- Views the world as unsafe and untrustworthy.

Other behaviours:

- Has difficulty with cause and effect.
- Steals or is deceitful.
- Acts controlling or bossy.
- Is manipulative.
- Displays sexual acting out behaviours.
- Refuses to do assignments or does them poorly.
- Speaks nonsensically, 'jabbers', slurs words or mumbles.
- Displays superficial and phoney behaviour.
- Shows abnormal eating patterns – either gorging or starving.
- Often prefers to be alone; does not do well in groups.
- Has difficulty understanding how their behaviour affects others and shows a lack of empathy.
- Has poor impulse control.
- Has physical aggression tendencies, injuring animals or other people.
- When distressed bangs their head; scratches, bites or cut themselves; or rocks back and forth.

Strategies to help a student with reactive attachment disorder

- Build positive relationships through establishing rapport and talking to the student about interests.

- Build self-esteem whenever possible in the classroom.
- Role model emotions, how to react to situations.
- Provide scenario training where possible.
- Identify difficult situations for the student and use a buddy or support person to assist in these times.
- Look for patterns of behaviours and use strategies based on the patterns.
- Teach anger management strategies such as rating anger out of ten or having a safe place to go.
- Modify work so student can achieve success and feel good about learning.
- Be very clear and consistent about rules and behaviour.
- Play games that have winning and losing and teach appropriate behaviours/reactions.
- Use charts with lots of different facial expressions/emotions on them to teach responses to situations.
- Correct with kindness when the student responds inappropriately.
- Communicate with parents/caregivers and external professionals regarding progress and observations.

Appendix 4

Ideas for Dylan

Here are some of my ideas to help Dylan at school and at home:

- Provide a clean uniform for Dylan to change into at school. School staff could volunteer to wash Dylan's uniform.
- Ensure Dylan has food for lunch and break. Provide healthy snacks such as fruit if needed.
- Provide Dylan with a toothbrush and teach him how to brush his teeth, wash his hands and face and how to brush his hair.
- Provide social skills training for Dylan in a small group.
- Provide life skills training for Dylan in how to care for himself. Be careful not to embarrass Dylan in the process. This must be done in a kind and caring manner.
- Partner Dylan with kind and caring students in the classroom.
- Give Dylan an opportunity to play games with peers so he can learn about taking turns, winning and losing, and cooperating with peers. Teach Dylan the rules of games prior to putting him into a group situation.
- Work with Dylan to improve coordination and balance. Consider where Dylan sits in the classroom and his walkways in and out of the classroom from his desk.
- Improve Dylan's organisation by minimising what he needs on his desk to get through the school day.
- Focus on Dylan's strengths in the classroom.
- Continue communication with father on a regular basis about Dylan's progress at school.
- Encourage Dylan into community or school-based extra-curricular activities that he can enjoy with peers.
- Look to involve outside agencies that can support Dylan.

Dylan will need a kind and caring approach from all of the staff members.

Appendix 5

Student information questionnaire

This questionnaire will need to be varied depending on the age of the student and family circumstances. Students can also include photos of family or pets as a part of the questionnaire.

Name:

Date of birth:

Family members:

Pets:

Favourite colour:

Sports played:

Musical instrument played:

Favourite food:

Favourite song/group:

Favourite sporting team:

Favourite game to play on the computer:

Job I want to do when I leave school:

Complete the statement: At school this year I want to achieve _____
_____

An alternative is: When I return to a school reunion I want to be remembered as _____

In order to achieve this I aim to _____
_____

Appendix 6

Sentence completion test

Name: _____

Sex: _____ Date of birth: _____

School: _____

Year: _____ Date: _____

1 I like _____

2 The happiest time _____

3 I want to know _____

4 At home _____

5 At night time _____

6 I am sorry for _____

7 The best _____

8 Boys _____

9 What upsets me _____

10 People _____

11 A mother _____

12 I feel _____

13 My greatest fear _____

14 In my previous school _____

15 I can't _____

16 Sports _____

17 When I was younger _____

18 My nerves _____

19 Other pupils _____

20 I suffer _____

21 I failed _____

22 Reading _____

23 My mind _____

24 The future _____

25 I need _____

26 Examinations are _____

27 I am best when _____

28 Sometimes _____

29 What annoys me _____

30 I hate _____

31 At school _____

32 I am very _____

33 The only trouble _____

34 I wish _____

35 My father _____

36 I secretly _____

37 Writing is _____

38 Dancing _____

39 My greatest worry is _____

40 Most girls _____

41 Facebook _____

42 The computer _____

Appendix 7

Ways to help students line up

Here are a number of ideas to help students line up. The ideas can vary depending of the ages of the students.

One of the first strategies is to make it a competition and this can be for house points, team points or my favourite, teacher versus class. In teacher versus class the class can only win and if they beat the challenge, the class receives some time to choose an activity in the afternoon or on Friday afternoon.

1 Have the students line up on spots in a designated space.
2 Have four lines for students to line up on in designated spaces.
3 Let the students choose where they line up on the spots.
4 Students can gather and then the teacher chooses where they line up and this is timed as a challenge.
5 Students gather and the teacher calls out the category for lining up. This category could be based on height, date of birth, favourite colour, football team premiership order etc. I find the students love this as it makes for a good timed challenge.
6 Students just gather and don't line up.

The important thing to solve the issue of problems in the line is for the teacher to be there early, just before the bell rings. That way the teacher can supervise. Now this seems unpleasant for a teacher as it means giving up some break time. However, in the long run it saves time as issues do not need to be sorted out upon entering the classroom.

The key is to make it fun, be creative for older children, and create a structure for younger children.

Index

Note: italics denote figures.